Doggin' Atlanta

The 50 Best Places To Hike With Your Dog In North Georgia

DOUG GELBERT

illustrations by

ANDREW CHESWORTH

CRUDEN BAY BOOKS

There is always a new trail to look forward to...

DOGGIN' ATLANTA: THE 50 BEST PLACES TO HIKE
WITH YOUR DOG IN NORTH GEORGIA

Cruden Bay Books
PO Box 467
Montchanin, DE 19710
www.hikewithyourdog.com

International Standard Book Number 978-1-935771-20-3

*"Dogs are our link to paradise...to sit with a dog on a hillside
on a glorious afternoon is to be back in Eden,
where doing nothing was not boring - it was peace."*
- Milan Kundera

Ahead On The Trail

Introduction

Atlanta can be a great place to hike with your dog. Within a short drive your canine adventurer can be climbing mountains that leave him panting, trotting through impossibly green ravines, exploring some of America's most historic ground or circling lakes for miles and never lose sight of the water.

I have selected what I consider to be the 50 best places to take your dog for an outing around Atlanta and ranked them according to subjective criteria including the variety of hikes available, opportunities for canine swimming and pleasure of the walks. The rankings include a mix of parks that feature long walks and parks that contain short walks. Did I miss your favorite? Let us know at *www.hikewithyourdog. com*.

For dog owners it is important to realize that not all parks are open to our best trail companions (see page 14 for a list of parks that do not allow dogs). It is sometimes hard to believe but not everyone loves dogs. We are, in fact, in the minority when compared with our non-dog owning neighbors.

So when visiting a park always keep your dog under control and clean up any messes and we can all expect our great parks to remain open to our dogs. And maybe some others will see the light as well. *Remember, every time you go out with your dog you are an ambassador for all dog owners.*

Grab that leash and hit the trail!
DBG

Hiking With Your Dog

So you want to start hiking with your dog. Hiking with your dog can be a fascinating way to explore the Atlanta region from a canine perspective. Some things to consider:

🐾 Dog's Health

Hiking can be a wonderful preventative for any number of physical and behavioral disorders. One in every three dogs is overweight and running up trails and leaping through streams is great exercise to help keep pounds off. Hiking can also relieve boredom in a dog's routine and calm dogs prone to destructive habits. And hiking with your dog strengthens the overall owner/dog bond.

🐾 Breed of Dog

All dogs enjoy the new scents and sights of a trail. But some dogs are better suited to hiking than others. If you don't as yet have a hiking companion, select a breed that matches your interests. Do you look forward to an entire afternoon's hiking? You'll need a dog bred to keep up with such a pace, such as a retriever or a spaniel. Is a half-hour enough walking for you? It may not be for an energetic dog like a border collie. If you already have a hiking friend, tailor your plans to his abilities.

🐾 Conditioning

Just like humans, dogs need to be acclimated to the task at hand. An inactive dog cannot be expected to bounce from the easy chair in the den to complete a 3-hour hike. You must also be physically able to restrain your dog if confronted with distractions on the trail (like a scampering squirrel or a pack of joggers). Have your dog checked by a veterinarian before significantly increasing his activity level.

🐾 Weather

Hot humid summers do not do dogs any favors. With no sweat glands and only panting available to disperse body heat, dogs are much more susceptible to heat stroke than we are. Unusually rapid panting and/or a bright red tongue are signs of heat exhaustion in your pet.

Always carry enough water for your hike. Even the prime hiking days of late fall through early spring that don't seem too warm can cause discomfort in dark-coated dogs if the sun is shining brightly. During cold snaps, short-coated breeds may require additional attention.

🐾 Trail Hazards

Dogs won't get poison ivy but they can transfer it to you. Some trails are littered with small pieces of broken glass that can slice a dog's paws. Nasty thorns can also blanket trails that we in shoes may never notice.

🐾 Ticks

You won't be able to spend much time in Georgia woods without encountering ticks. All are nasty but the deer tick - no bigger than a pin head - carries with it the spectre of Lyme disease. Lyme disease attacks a dog's joints and makes walking painful. The tick needs to be embedded in the skin to transmit Lyme disease. It takes 4-6 hours for a tick to become embedded and another 24-48 hours to transmit Lyme disease bacteria.

When hiking, walk in the middle of trails away from tall grass and bushes. And when the summer sun fades away don't stop thinking about ticks - they remain active any time the temperature is above 30 degrees. By checking your dog - and yourself - thoroughly after each walk you can help avoid Lyme disease. Ticks tend to congregate on your dog's ears, between the toes and around the neck and head.

🐾 Water

Surface water, including fast-flowing streams, is likely to be infested with a microscopic protozoa called *Giardia*, waiting to wreak havoc on a dog's intestinal system. The most common symptom is crippling diarrhea. Algae, pollutants and contaminants can all be in streams, ponds and puddles. If possible, carry fresh water for your dog on the trail - your dog can even learn to drink happily from a squirt bottle.

🐾 Rattlesnakes and Copperheads, etc.

Rattlesnakes and their close cousins, copperheads, are not particularly aggressive animals but you should treat any venomous snake with respect and keep your distance. A rattler's colors may vary but they are recognized by the namesake rattle on the tail and a diamond-shaped head. Unless cornered or teased by humans or dogs, a rattlesnake will crawl away and avoid striking. Avoid placing your hand in unexamined rocky areas and crevasses and try and keep your dog from putting his nose in such places as well. Stick to the trail and out of high grass where you can't see well. If you hear a nearby rattle, stop immediately and hold your dog back. Identify where the snake is and slowly back away.

If you or your dog is bitten, do not panic but get to a hospital or veterinarian with as little physical movement as possible. Wrap between the bite and the heart. Rattlesnakes might give "dry bites" where no poison is injected, but you should always check with a doctor after a bite even if you feel fine.

🐾 Porcupines

Porcupines are easy for a curious dog to catch and that makes them among the most dangerous animals you may meet because an embedded quill is not only painful but can cause infection if not properly removed.

⦚ **Black Bears**

Are you likely to see a bear while out hiking with your dog? No, it's not likely. It is, however, quite a thrill if you are fortunate enough to spot a black bear on the trail - from a distance.

Black bear attacks are incredibly rare. In the year 2000 a hiker was killed by a black bear in Great Smoky National Park and it was the first deadly bear attack in the 66-year history of America's most popular national park. It was the first EVER in the southeastern United States. In all of North America only 43 black bear mauling deaths have ever been recorded (through 1999).

Most problems with black bears occur near a campground (like the above incident) where bears have learned to forage for unprotected food. On the trail bears will typically see you and leave the area. What should you do if you encounter a black bear? Experts agree on three important things:

1) Never run. A bear will outrun you, outclimb you, outswim you. Don't look like prey.
2) Never get between a female bear and a cub who may be nearby feeding.
3) Leave a bear an escape route.

If the bear is at least 15 feet away and notices you make sure you keep your dog close and calm. If a bear stands on its hind legs or comes closer it may just be trying to get a better view or smell to evaluate the situation. Wave your arms and make noise to scare the bear away. Most bears will quickly leave the area.

If you encounter a black bear at close range, stand upright and make yourself appear as large a foe as possible. Avoid direct eye contact and speak in a calm, assertive and assuring voice as you back up slowly and out of danger.

Outfitting Your Dog For A Hike

These are the basics for taking your dog on a hike:

- **Collar.**
  A properly fitting collar should not be so loose as to come off but you should be able to slide your flat hand under the collar.

- **Identification Tags.**
  Get one with your veterinarian's phone number as well.

- **Bandanna.**
  Can help distinguish him from game in hunting season.

- **Leash.**
  Leather lasts forever but if there's water in your dog's future, consider quick-drying nylon.

- **Water.**
  Carry 8 ounces for every hour of hiking.

I want my dog to help carry water, snacks and other supplies on the trail. Where do I start?

To select an appropriate dog pack measure your dog's girth around the rib cage. A dog pack should fit securely without hindering the dog's ability to walk normally.

Will my dog wear a pack?

Wearing a dog pack is no more obtrusive than wearing a collar, although some dogs will take to a pack easier than others. Introduce the pack by draping a towel over your dog's back in the house and then having your dog wear an empty pack on short walks. Progressively add some crumpled newspaper and then bits of clothing. Fill the pack with treats and reward your dog from the stash. Soon your dog will associate the dog pack with an outdoor adventure and will eagerly look forward to wearing it.

🐾 *How much weight can I put into a dog pack?*

Many dog packs are sold by weight recommendations. A healthy, well-conditioned dog can comfortably carry 25% to 33% of its body weight. Breeds prone to back problems or hip dysplasia should not wear dog packs. Consult your veterinarian before stuffing the pouches with gear.

🐾 *How does a dog wear a pack?*

The pack, typically with cargo pouches on either side, should ride as close to the shoulders as possible without limiting movement. The straps that hold the dog pack in place should be situated where they will not cause chafing.

🐾 *What are good things to put in a dog pack?*

Low density items such as food and poop bags are good choices. Ice cold bottles of water can cool your dog down on hot days. Don't put anything in a dog pack that can break. Dogs will bang the pack on rocks and trees as they wiggle through tight spots in the trail. Dogs also like to lie down in creeks and other wet spots so seal items in plastic bags. A good use for dog packs when on day hikes around North Georgia is trail maintenance - your dog can pack out trash left by inconsiderate visitors before you.

🐾 *Are dog booties a good idea?*

Although not typically necessary, dog booties can be an asset, especially for the occasional canine hiker whose paw pads have not become toughened. Trails can be rocky and in some places there may be broken glass or roots. Hiking boots for dogs are designed to prevent pads from cracking while trotting across rough surfaces.

🐾 *What should a doggie first aid kit include?*

Even when taking short hikes it is a good idea to have some basics available for emergencies:

- ▶ 4" square gauze pads
- ▶ cling type bandaging tapes
- ▶ topical wound disinfectant cream
- ▶ tweezers
- ▶ insect repellent - no reason to leave your dog unprotected against mosquitoes and biting flies
- ▶ veterinarian's phone number

The Other End Of The Leash

Leash laws are like speed limits - everyone seems to have a private interpretation of their validity. Some dog owners never go outside with an unleashed dog; others treat the laws as suggestions or disregard them completely. It is not the purpose of this book to tell dog owners where to go to evade the leash laws or reveal the parks where rangers will look the other way at an unleashed dog. Nor is it the business of this book to preach vigilant adherence to the leash laws. Nothing written in a book is going to change people's behavior with regard to leash laws. So this will be the last time leash laws are mentioned, save occasionally when we point out the parks where dogs are welcomed off leash.

Low Impact Hiking With Your Dog

Every time you hike with your dog on the trail you are an ambassador for all dog owners. Some people you meet won't believe in your right to take a dog on the trail. Be friendly to all and make the best impression you can by practicing low impact hiking with your dog:

- Pack out everything you pack in.

- Do not leave dog scat on the trail; if you haven't brought plastic bags for poop removal bury it away from the trail and topical water sources.

- Hike only where dogs are allowed.

- Stay on the trail.

- Do not allow your dog to chase wildlife.

- Step off the trail and wait with your dog while horses and other hikers pass.

- Do not allow your dog to bark - people are enjoying the trail for serenity.

- *Have as much fun on your hike as your dog does.*

The Best of the Best

🐾 **BEST CANINE HIKE TO A VIEW**
Rabun Bald

🐾 **BEST HIKE TO MEET OTHER DOGS**
Chattahoochee River NRA-Cochran Shoals

🐾 **BEST HIKE TO NOT SEE ANOTHER DOG**
Crockford-Pigeon Mountain WMA

🐾 **BEST 1-HOUR WORKOUT FOR YOUR DOG**
Burnt Mountain Preserve

🐾 **BEST CANINE HIKE TO A WATERFALL**
Raven Cliffs Fall

🐾 **BEST PARK TO SWIM WITH YOUR DOG**
Murphey Candler Park

🐾 **BEST HIKE TO CIRCLE A LAKE WITH YOUR DOG**
Unicoi State Park - Unicoi Lake

🐾 **BEST PLACE TO HIKE ALL DAY WITH YOUR DOG**
Cloudland State Park

🐾 **PRETTIEST HIKE WITH YOUR DOG**
Red Top Mountain State Park-Homestead Trail

🐾 **MOST HISTORIC HIKE WITH YOUR DOG**
Allatoona Pass Battlefield

No Dogs

Before we get started on the best places to take your dog, let's get out of the way some of the parks that do not allow dogs at all:

Buford Dam Park - Buford
Burton Mill Park - Flowery Branch
Chattahoochee Nature Center - Roswell
Fernbank Forest and Recreation Center - Atanta
Panola Mountain State Conservation Park - Stockbridge
Sawnee Mountain Preserve - Cumming
State Botanical Gardens of Georgia - Athens

O.K. that wasn't too bad. Let's forget about these and move on to some of the great places where we CAN take our dogs on Atlanta area trails...

The 50 Best Places To Hike With Your Dog Around Atlanta...

Red Top Mountain State Park

The Park

Red Top Mountain comes by its name honestly - just under the topsoil is an abundance of iron ore that tints Georgia's dirt a reddish color. Some of America's first industries, and corresponding fortunes, were made by ironmasters in the hills of Pennsylvania. A descendant of that ironmaking tradition, Jacob Stroup, arrived in North Georgia in 1836 and built his first blast furnace on the banks of nearby Stamp Creek. Prior to the Civil War there would be at least nine furnaces producing iron slag in Bartow County with its center at the town of Etowah, started by Stroup. The Etowah Manufacturing and Mining Company grew into the second largest corporation in the Deep South with over 500 workers in its employ. But Bartow County's iron industry was destroyed by Union troops in 1864 and never revived.

In the 1940s - in the name of flood control, hydroelectric power generation, water supply, fish management and recreation - the U.S. Army Corps of Engineers impounded the Etowah River and created Lake Allatoona with 270 miles of shoreline. Underneath its 12,000 acres are the remains of the town of Etowah. Today Lake Allatoona hosts more than six million visitors, making it some years the most visited Corps of Engineers lake in America.

Bartow County	
Phone Number	
- (770) 975-0055	
Website	
- gastateparks.org/ RedTopMountain	
Admission Fee	
- $5 parking fee	
Park Hours	
- 7 AM - 10 PM	
Directions	
- *Cartersville*; 50 Lodge Road. From I-75 take Exit 285 east for 1.5 miles into the park.	

The Walks

The marquee canine hike in Red Top Mountain is the 3.5-mile *Homestead Trail* loop that is accessed from the Visitor Center with a 20-minute walk or the Lodge area with a 10-minute walk. This is one of Atlanta's most beautiful trails - wide, moderately graded, piney and in the almost constant company of the lake - as it ducks in and out of the fingers of water created by the flooding of the Etowah River. If you use the Visitor Center access, mix the *Homestead Trail* with the *Sweet Gum Trail* for a superb canine hiking outing. Also leaving from the Lodge area are quick leg-stretcher trails that hug the lake as well. The *Iron Hill Trail* takes advantage of an old mining road to venture out to an abandoned 50-foot deep open-cut iron mine. Your dog will find gravel under paw much of the nearly four miles here, as befits a trail that was designated for mountain bikes.

Trail Sense: Excellent park maps and even though you will scarcely need it you will almost always see a blaze as you hike with your dog at Red Top Mountain - if only some of Georgia's more remote trails were as diligent.

Dog Friendliness
Dogs are allowed on the park trails and in the campground.

Traffic
Bikes are not allowed on the main hiking trails.

Canine Swimming
Your dog can easily slip down from the *Homestead Trail* for some dog paddling in Lake Allatoona or find a swim in the lots by the lake.

Trail Time
More than an hour.

2
Sweetwater Creek State Park

The Park

Charles James McDonald, who had just completed a four-year stint as the 37th governor of Georgia, bought land along the Sweetwater Creek in 1845 for $500. With his partner, Colonel James Rogers of Milledgeville, McDonald set out to put the energetic waters of the creek to use by building a textile mill. By late 1849 the Sweetwater Manufacturing Company was churning out cotton, yarn, and fabric. The business thrived and in 1858 McDonald renamed his mill after the center of the British textile industry in Manchester, England. During the Civil War the New Manchester Manufacturing Company attracted the attention of Union General William Tecumseh Sherman's troops who destroyed the mills on July 9, 1864. The business was never revived and the 1,986- acre Sweetwater Creek State Park was founded to protect the brick ruins of the historic factory.

Douglas County

Phone Number
- (770) 732-5871

Website
- gastateparks.org/ SweetwaterCreek

Admission Fee
- $5 parking fee

Park Hours
- 7 AM - 10 PM daily

Directions
- *Lithia Springs*; 1750 Mt. Vernon Road. From I-20 use Exit 44 at Thornton Road and head south, getting into the right lane as soon as possible. After a 1/4-mile, turn right on Blairs Bridge Road at the sign. After 2 miles, turn left on Mount Vernon Road and continue to the third park entrance on the left, with parking at the trailhead.

The Walks

There are some nine miles of hiking trails on both sides of the Sweetwater Creek and the star is the red-blazed route that leads to the riverside factory ruins. This trail serves up a bit of everything for your dog from a ramble down the remants of the road that served the town that grew up around the mill to a pick-your-way exercise through rocky outcoppings above the river.

Bonus

At five stories, the New Manchester Mill was said to be the tallest building built in the Atlanta area before the Civil War. A 25-ton water wheel powered all the operations in the factory, which employed as many as 100 workers. Today the raceway and the stately ruins are the only reminders of this chapter in the region's history.

The town was once a bustling place where as many as 400 people lived, large enough to merit its own post office but no trace remains today. Past the ruins wooden steps drop you to the water's edge and eventually the cascades of Sweetwater Falls. The inland *Blue Nature Trail* closes a loop back to the trailhead by moving easily up and around the hills above the creek.

The sporty *Yellow Trail* traipses through similar terrain across the creek on a three-mile loop. A natural highlight is a wide, 10-foot shelf of rocky outcropping known as the "Indian Cave."

The park boasts some of Atlanta's most impressive Civil War ruins.

Trail Sense: A park map is available, key junctions are marked and detailed descriptions of each trail, including length and terrain, are posted at the trailheads.

Dog Friendliness
Dogs are welcome at Sweetwater Creek and you can usually find a bowl of drinking water outside the Visitor Center. The park also conducts monthly ranger-led "Wagging Trails" hikes.

Traffic
Foot traffic only on the trails.

Canine Swimming
The rock-studded shoals of Sweetwater Creek, with Class IV rapids, is no place for extended canine aquatics but your dog can step in and cool off safely in a few spots, including a stony beach and generous pool between the Factory Ruins and the Sweetwater Falls Overlook.

Trail Time
A half-day of canine hiking and expect any outing to occupy at least an hour.

3

Cloudland State Park

The Park

To geologists, the impressive gash in the limestone at the western end of Lookout Mountain was Trenton Gulch. Locals knew the 1,000-foot deep gorge as Sitton Gulch. After the Civilian Conservation Corps arrived in the 1930s to carve the first access roads into the area from Georgia the newly designated state park was bestowed with the more beguiling name of Cloudland Canyon for its opening in 1939. The state acquired enough land to create a sprawling park of 1,924 acres; today the boundaries have almost doubled.

Dade County

Phone Number
- (706) 657-4050

Website
- gastateparks.org/
CloudlandCanyon

Admission Fee
- $5 parking fee

Park Hours
- 7 AM - 10 PM daily

Directions
- *Trenton*; six miles east of town on the north side of GA 136. Approached from the east, 18 miles west of LaFayette.

The Walks

Cloudland Canyon serves up some of the most dramatic hiking in North Georgia and your dog can experience every step of it. The best walk is the *West Rim Loop Trail* that covers about three miles and follows up visits to canyon overlooks with views of the town of Trenton down the western slope. For the full flavor

Sheer cliffs surround your dog in Cloudland Canyon.

of this scenic trail begin your dog's journey on the East Rim and use the connector trail across Daniel Creek. Don't let the scenery distract your dog here - the undulating route hugs unprotected ledges as it rolls along.

One thing your dog won't see on the *West Rim Trail* are the park's stunning waterfalls, 60-foot Cherokee Falls and 90-foot Hemlock Falls. To get face-to-face with these hydro-spectaculars requires conquering 600 steps into the canyon (the Washington Monument has 897 steps). These steps are of the open-grate variety which will abort the trip for some dogs. If you make it to the canyon floor your dog can test *Sitton's Gulch Loop Trail* that runs five miles out the north end of the gorge.

Your dog's reward for scrambling down steep stairways is the picturesque plunge of Cherokee Falls.

If you are spending the weekend at Cloudland Canyon there is additional canine hiking in the park's backcountry. A shorter loop traipses through haughty stands of hemlock and a longer spur that covers nine miles drops down to Bear Creek.

Trail Sense: Park signs point the way at critical junctions.

Dog Friendliness
Dogs are allowed on the trails and in the campground.
Traffic
Foot traffic in and around the gorge.
Canine Swimming
Seasonal streams provide a refreshing spash as they flow across the plateau on the *West Rim Trail* before they drop into the canyon.
Trail Time
Several hours to a full weekend possible.

4
Fort Mountain
State Park

The Park

The Woodland Indians inhabited this area for more than a thousand years until about 900 AD. Traces of their civilization have been uncovered in mounds, petroglyphs and structures such as the "wall of stone" that stretches for nearly three football fields along the top of this mountain. Early discoverers assumed it was an ancient fort, hence the park name, but it is now believed to have been of ceremonial origins since the low walls would have provided minimal protection and there was no source of water within its boundaries to sustain defenders. But no one knows for sure how the wall got here, giving rise to legends from wandering Welsh explorers who pre-date Christopher Columbus to Cherokee tales of spectral builders known as "Moon Eyes." In 1926 the crest of Fort Mountain was purchased by Ivan Allen with plans to construct a resort. Allen, who began his career peddling typewriters and built the largest office supply house in the South, was the first president of the Atlanta Convention Bureau and considered the town's leading booster. Allen scrapped his development plans and instead donated the first land to the State of Georgia for the 3,268-acre park.

Murray County

Phone Number
- (706) 422-1932

Website
- gastateparks.org/FortMountain

Admission Fee
- $5 parking fee

Park Hours
- 7 AM - 10 PM daily

Directions
- *Chatsworth*; eight miles east of town on GA 52. Take Exit 333 off I-75 east through Chatsworth.

The Walks

Fort Mountain offers a pleasing mix of short and long hikes that will set any dog's tail to wagging. Your first stop will likely be the series of short trails leading up to the summit of the 2,832-foot mountain - any combination can be used to reach the attractions of a west-facing overlook, observation tower and the mysterious stone wall.

Bonus

While the origins of the mountain's stone wall are shrouded in mystery the builders of the well-crafted 38-foot stone observation tower are well documented. The Civilian Conservation Corps erected it in the 1930s. Find a heart-shaped stone implant in the east window.

Next up for your dog will be the 17-acre Fort Mountain Lake where an easy trot will cover the 1.2 wooded miles around the water. Across the road is the sporty half-mile *Big Rock Nature Trail* that loops between two cascading streams, including the 400-foot Gold Mine Creek Falls.

At this time the park observation tower is more for looking at than looking from.

Seasoned canine hikers will want to block out a half-day at Fort Mountain to tackle the 8.2-mile *Gahuti Trail* that loops around the mountain. One of the premiere treks in the state park system, the orange-blazed *Gahuti* rambles to outstanding views as it weaves its way through the Virginia pines and gnarled oaks clinging to the hillsides.

Trail Sense: Park trails are well-blazed and a the detailed color maps produced by the state park system can be found at the Visitor Center.

Dog Friendliness
Dogs are welcome on the trails and in the campground; two of the park cottages are dog-friendly.

Traffic
Mountain bikers and equestrians have their own trails around the park.

Canine Swimming
Dogs can't use the beach at the park lake but there is easy access to dog paddling from the *Lake Trail*.

Trail Time
Several hours to a full day of hiking on tap for your dog here.

5
Kennesaw Mountain National Battlefield Park

The Park

By the spring of 1864 Atlanta was the great prize of the Civil War, both strategically and politically. Its railroads and foundries made it a critical Confederate center for making war and if the approaching Union offensive ordered by General Ulysses S. Grant could be repelled there was every possibility that Abraham Lincoln would be defeated in the fall election by George McClellan who would likely end the war by preserving the existence of the Confederacy.

Union General William T. Sherman launched his Atlanta Campaign from Chattanooga in early May and by mid-June only the imposing Confederate defenses on Kennesaw Mountain stood between his army and Atlanta. Sherman employed persistent flanking maneuvers - and one disastrous frontal assault - over the course of two weeks of fighting. The Northerners surrendered men but the Confederates surrendered ground, eventually abandoning their positions on Kennesaw Mountain on the night of July 2. Sherman crossed the Chattahoochee River and laid siege to Atlanta which capitulated on September 2.

Cobb County

Phone Number
- (770) 427-4686

Website
- nps.gov/kemo

Admission Fee
- None

Park Hours
- Dawn to dusk

Directions
- *Kennesaw*; northwest of Marietta. From Exit 269 of I-75 take Barrett Parkway west for 2.1 miles. Turn left on Old 41 Highway and go 1.2 miles to Stilesboro Road on the right. Turn and make the immediate left into the Visitor Center lot.

The Walks

This is one of the most popular canine hiking spots in the Atlanta area. The NPS and the Kennesaw Mountain Trail Club maintain over 20 miles of trails that flow south of the Visitor Center. The trail system is essentially three loops divided by the busy east-west roads that sever the battlefield.

Many dog walkers climb up the paved park road (closed to vehicles on the weekend), a trip of about one mile with an elevation gain of over 650 feet and east-facing views to Atlanta. The summit of Kennesaw Mountain reveals the defensive strength of the Confederate position over the surrounding countryside and why Sherman concentrated his efforts to moving to the

Confederate defensive positions atop Kennesaw Mountain.

south. The return to the Visitor Center can be accomplished back down the road or via a wooded trail that moves past historic entrenchments. A full exploration of the mountain for your dog that will stay off the park road and include Pigeon Hill will cover an ambitious loop of over six miles.

The loops south of the mountain at Cheatham Hill and Kolb's Farm, where the fiercest fighting occurred in June 1864, serve up easier hiking for your dog on well-maintained natural paths. A loop of the entire 2,884-acre battlefield requires 17 miles for those dogs up to the challenge.

Trail Sense: A park map and trail map with distances can be retrieved from the Visitor Center; also a cell phone audio tour.

Dog Friendliness
Dogs are welcome at Kennesaw Mountain and poop bags are provided.
Traffic
Foot travel only, except on the park road during the week.
Canine Swimming
The trails cross a few streams but this is a canine hiking park.
Trail Time
At least an hour and up to a full day.

6
Chattahoochee River NRA-East Palisades

The Park

Most rivers meander and change course over time but the Chattahoochee River is locked in place by the 320-mile Brevard Fault that divides the Appalachian Mountains and the Piedmont Plateau. As such, it is one of the oldest rivers in America. President Jimmy Carter created the Chattahoochee River National Recreation Area in his home state to protect 48 miles of the slow-moving waters south of Lake Lanier. Today the 4,100-acre preserve is one of the most popular destinations in the national park system, attracting more than three million visitors each year. The East Palisades is the southernmost of the park service's 14 units; the rugged granite cliffs that rise 400 feet above the river were called the Devil's Stairsteps by boatmen because the shoals "were the devil" to navigate.

Fulton County

Phone Number
- (678) 538-1200

Website
- nps.gov/chat

Admission Fee
- Parking fee

Park Hours
- Sunrise to sunset

Directions
- *Atlanta*; Indian Trail entrance: take Exit 22 off I-285 and follow Northside Drive as it winds south. After passing Old Powers Road on the left, go 1.1 miles and turn right on Indian Trail to parking area. Whitewater Creek entrance: go another half-mile to Harris Trail and turn right on Whitewater Creek Road to the entrance on the right.

The Walks

In the shadow of one of America's busiest highways and in the flight path of a major air force base your dog can still find sporty trails that will set her tail to wagging and her tongue to panting. Using the entrance road for a short jaunt, you can fashion a three-to-four mile loop that drops to the river level and picks its way to top of the Palisades. There are numerous routes to choose from but the short trail segments are all a mile away from the trailhead. The destination for most canine hikers will be a wooden observation

From the observation deck your dog can enjoy a panoramic view of the tannin-tinted brown river - and upstream a reminder that you are not far from civilization on the Palisades.

deck that is perched over a signature bend in the Chattahoochee River.

Trail Sense: There is a mapboard in the parking lot and "You Are Here" maps posted at trail junctions which are useful when the trail system gets tangled at the top of the Palisades.

Dog Friendliness

Dogs are welcome to trot these trails.

Traffic

Some fishermen but mostly hikers; no bikes permitted.

Canine Swimming

When the trail reaches the banks of the Chattahoochee River it offers some of the best swimming access for your dog in the entire 14 units - the banks are low and the water relatively calm. Don't forget the water temperature rarely gets above 50 degrees in the river.

Trail Time

At least an hour once you point your dog to the trailhead.

7
Raven
Cliffs Falls

The Park

The designation of nearly 10,000 acres as "wilderness" does not scare off many folks at Raven Cliffs - the five-mile round trip to the falls is one of the most hiked trails within striking distance of Atlanta. In 1912, the Byrd-Matthews Lumber Company built a great sawmill in the flat land at Robertstown and constructed a narrow gauge railroad to haul trees off the mountain along Dodd Creek to feed the mill. That old roadbed is what your dog will be walking on along here.

The Walks

If you have ever hunted waterfalls with your dog in a national forest you

White County

Phone Number
- (706) 754-6221

Website
- fs.usda.gov/conf

Admission Fee
- None

Park Hours
- Sunrise to sunset

Directions
- *Chattahoochee National Forest;* west of Helen. North of town turn left on GA 75 Alternate. After 2.3 miles turn right at the sign for the Richard B. Russell Scenic Highway. The parking area for Raven Cliffs is three miles on the left.

know that there is never a sign that identifies the sought-after falls. If there was ever the need for a "THIS IS IT!" sign, it is at Raven Cliffs Falls. Dodd Creek deals out so many hydrospectaculars in the form of sluices, cascades and waterfalls that tumbling water downstream from Raven Cliffs could easily pass for your destination. And would qualify as a satisfying canine hike if you were to mistakenly stop and turn around on the out-and-back trail.

Even so, keep going until you can go no further. And then go a little further, following your dog up a 40-foot scramble to see a water spout crashing down a crevasse behind two massive blocks of stone. That is Raven Cliffs Falls. The entire canine hike is about 2.5 miles, one way. Dodd Creek is seldom out of sight and its roar never out of earshot. Save for a few tricky passages, this is easy trotting for your dog the entire way. There are also unprotected drop-offs above the stream so take extra care with a spirited trail dog.

Trail Sense: The trailhead is between the small bridge you crossed on the road in and the parking lot - that is your most difficult wayfinding task here.

Dog Friendliness
Dogs are welcome on this popular national forest trail.

Traffic
Foot travel only but expect company on this canine hike any weekend.

Canine Swimming
There are a few places to stop for a doggie dip when the waters of Dodd Creek runs high. Early on, below the trail there is a large pool where the stream makes a 90-degree turn and about a mile into hike where the trail falls into Dodd Creek the water collects in a small, but deep pool that makes a superb canine swimming hole.

Trail Time
Two to three hours to reach the falls and return.

This is the real Raven Cliffs Falls - don't be fooled by impressive imposters like this...

8
Chickamauga Battlefield

The Park

In 1863, the grand military prize of the Civil War was the railroad center of Chattanooga, known as the "Gateway to the Deep South." The Confederates carried the day in September fighting here but a flood of Union reinforcements that arrived a month later defeated the rebel forces in Chattanooga and set the stage for the devastating Atlanta campaign. In 1890 Congress authorized the establishment of the first four national military parks: Shiloh, Gettysburg, Vicksburg and Chickamauga & Chattanooga, the first and largest.

Catoosa County

Phone Number
- (706) 866-9241

Website
- nps.gov/chch

Admission Fee
- None

Park Hours
- Grounds open sunrise to sunset

Directions
- *Fort Oglethorpe*; at 3370 LaFayette Road. Take Exit 350 off I-75 west on Highway 2 (Battlefield Parkway). In town turn left on La-Fayette Road to the Visitor Center.

The Walks

More than many battlefields Chickamauga has been developed as a recreational park with horse trails and hiking paths and picnic areas. There are over ten miles of trails, not including park roads and multi-use paths, with the *Equestrian Loop* circling the entire battlefield for over seven miles.

This is easy trotting for your dog through a gently rolling landscape. There are open fields but your canine hiking day will be spent mostly in the surrounding forests where most of the monuments and historical markers are found (there are 1,400 in the military park). Much of this landscape is little changed from the days of the Civil War.

The Park Service has also designed self-guided tours ranging in length from five miles to the all-encompassing 14-mile *Cannon Trail*, which after completing will surely leave your dog a Civil War scholar.

Snodgrass Hill, the scene of some of the most desperate fighting of the Civil War in Georgia is now a quiet place to relax with your dog.

Trail Sense: Pick up a trail map in addition to the park map as several short paths branch off the main routes, leading to points of interest.

Dog Friendliness
Dogs are welcome to use the paved and natural trails in the battlefield park.

Traffic
Depending on your chosen route you can be sharing the trails with bikes, horses or joggers - or have some of the lesser visited park areas to your dog and yourself.

Canine Swimming
Although not a prominent fature of the park, a determined dog can get a swim in Chickamauga Creek.

Trail Time
You can fashion any length of canine hike at Chickamauga from a short ramble to a lengthy, intensive exploration of the battlefield.

9
Chattahoochee River NRA-Gold Branch

The Park

Stephen Morgan Smith was North Carolina-born and Moravian College-educated in Bethlehem, Pennsylvania. After graduation he answered the call of the ministry and became a preacher until, in 1871 at the age of 32, throat problems ended his days of delivering sermons. Smith had no money and no prospects. While tinkering in his home he had invented a washing machine for family use and was astonished to discover a demand for the contraption. In 1877, Smith invented the world's first "S" turbine, installing it at a Pennsylvania grist mill and laying the foundation for one of 19th century America's most formidable industries.

In 1897 Smith came to Atlanta to install power plants with his turbines. He selected a narrow point on a bend in the Chattahoochee River and created the Atlanta Water and Electric Company. In 1904 the dam on Bull Sluice was operational, by far the largest hydroelectric plant in the state. But S. Morgan Smith did not live to see the first power generated from the project - he had died a year earlier of a heart attack while visiting California and the dam and 673-acre reservoir were named in his honor.

Cobb County
Phone Number - (678) 538-1200
Website - nps.gov/chat
Admission Fee - Parking fee
Park Hours - Sunrise to sunset
Directions - *Roswell*; south of town. Take Exit 24 off I-285 and follow Riverside Drive north to Johnson Ferry Road in 2.3 miles. Turn left and right on Lower Roswell Road. Continue to the park entrance on the right.

The Walks

This is some of the best woods walking you can do with your dog near the heart of Atlanta. This is a passive recreation park - there is nothing else to do at Gold Branch than to hike or have a bite to eat in the small picnic area. The trail system is a series of stacked loops that afford canine hikes of any desired duration from a half-hour to nearly two hours. Much of your dog's trotting will take place on wide trails that, not surprisingly, were old roadbeds when they were constructed. These trails bound over and around the hilly terrain, dropping down to lake level at points where the shoreline has been smoothed out for fishermen - and your water-loving dog.

Trail Sense: Mapboards are posted at the trail junctions.

Dog Friendliness

Dogs are welcome at Gold Branch and poop bags are provided.

Traffic

No bikes, foot traffic only.

Canine Swimming

Once your dog knows the way to the edge of Bull Sluice Lake there will be no holding her back.

Trail Time

Up to two hours possible.

Dogs who love to swim are likely to spend as much time in the water as on the trail at Gold Branch.

10
Sandy Creek
Nature Center

The Park

White clay for bricks was scraped from the banks of the Sandy Creek beginning in the early 1900s. The brick factory that operated here churned out building blocks used in area houses and on the campus of the University of Georgia. By mid-century the factory was abandoned and the kilns and chimneys were left to crumble into rubble. Nature reclaimed the industrial site and 225 acres were set aside and preserved as a wildlife sanctuary and environmental education facility.

The Walks

The trail system at Sandy Creek Nature Center covers four miles on

Clarke County

Phone Number
- (706) 613-3615

Website
- Athensclarkecounty.com/
sandycreeknaturecenter

Admission Fee
- None

Park Hours
- Trails open daily from sunrise to sunset

Directions
- *Athens*; 205 Old Commerce Road, north of town. Take Exit 12 off the Athens Perimeter north on Commerce Road (15/441). Make the first left on Nature Center Road and left to the parking lot.

a network of a dozen short trails that scoot off a wooded ridge into the floodplain of the North Oconee River and the wetlands along Sandy Creek. The centerpiece is the Claypit Pond, a deep gouge from the brick-making days that has filled with water and is now the home to beaver, frogs and turtles. The *Claypit Pond Trail* traces the shoreline for about a half-mile, winding past foundation ruins left by the Georgia Brick Company.

This is easy going for your dog on soft, dirt trails that extend in the park to the confluence of Sandy Creek and the North Oconee River. The low-lying trails can turn muddy and impassable after wet sessions but the pathways in the wooded uplands present a drier option on such days.

Sandy Creek Nature Center is also the terminus for a pair of linear paths: the paved *North Oconee River Greenway* that exits the southern half of the park and the natural surface *Cook's Trail* that links the Nature Center to Sandy Creek Park about four miles away. The two ends are the only access points to *Cook's Trail* so if you use a car shuttle be aware that Sandy Creek Park is gated. The route traipses leisurely through beaver swamps and lowlands under majestic hardwoods. A worthy destination for canine hikers not wishing to tackle the whole

Neither the Log House nor the woods at Sandy Creek Nature Center represent how this land looked for most of its history.

four miles is the *Oxbow Loop* about half-way down the trail. The mile-long path explores wetlands highlighted by a lush fernbank.

Trail Sense: An excellent printed map is available at the trailhead and signs mark the many trail junctions.

Dog Friendliness

Dogs are welcome on the Nature Center trails; at the trailhead poop bags are provided and there is a special doggie fountain. At Sandy Creek Park there is a one-acre dog park but dogs are not allowed on the beach or in Lake Chapman.

Traffic

Foot traffic only on the trails.

Canine Swimming

There are places along Sandy Creek and North Oconee River where your dog can slip down the bank for a swim.

Trail Time

More than an hour in the Nature Center and much more possible with a journey on *Cook's Trail.*

11
Amicalola Falls State Park

The Park

Although at 729 feet, the Amicalola Falls (the name is a derivation of the Cherokee word for "tumbling waters") are the highest cascading waterfall east of the Mississippi River they were not developed as a tourist attraction until the State of Georgia bought the land and made it their 12th state park in 1940. The Crane family, starting with Bartley Crane, had owned the land around the falls since 1852. The family rented some cabins and hosted the occasional religious camp meeting but mostly they ran a corn and flour mill along the creek a half-mile from the base of the falls.

Dawson County

Phone Number
- (706) 265-4703

Website
- gastateparks.org/AmicalolaFalls

Admission Fee
- $5 parking fee

Park Hours
- 7 AM - 10 PM daily

Directions
- *Dawsonville*; northwest of town. Follow I-575 north to the end and pick up Route 53 south. Turn left and go north on Route 183 to the junction of Route 52. Turn right and go east to the park entrance.

The *Appalachian Trail* originally ran through the park but the southern terminus was switched to Springer Mountain in 1958. Today an 8.5-mile approach trail links the base of the falls to the *Appalachian Trail* terminal and many thru-hikers begin their epic journeys here, at the closest paved road access to Springer Mountain.

The Walks

The falls are not just the centerpiece of one of Georgia's most popular parks - they are the only thing for most canine hikers. And the park service has given you a cornucopia of ways to experience the cascading water. The easiest, assuming you are not going to drive up to top of the falls, is to start at the Reflection Pool and climb up the paved approach trail to the Lower Observation Platform. A sportier chase would be to start in the parking lot across from the Visitor Center and hike the *Creek Trail* a half-mile to the access.

Once at the Lower Observation Platform your way up is via 175 open-grate steps. If your dog doesn't do open-grate steps, your exploration is over. Otherwise you will make it half-way up the falls. From here you can close your loop by hiking down the *West Ridge Falls Access*, the *Spring Trail* and the *Mt. Laurel Loop* back to the *Creek Trail*. If your athletic dog has not seen enough of Amicalola Falls you can climb to the top on 425 more steps

175 steps down, 425 to go.

and cross the creek to return along the one-mile *East Ridge Trail*, which was once the approach route to the *Appalachian Trail*. The steps are the wild card for your dog here - if they are going to be a problem approach the falls from the ridge trails on either side and go down the steps or go out-and-back.

Trail Sense: If all that wasn't as crystal clear as the waters in Little Amicalola Creek there are maps and trail signs galore to lead you around the park.

Dog Friendliness
Dogs are not allowed at the Hike Inn - Georgia's only backcountry lodge.
Traffic
The approaches to the falls are by foot, although wheelchairs and strollers can gain access from the West Ridge parking lot.
Canine Swimming
Your dog can cool down in the Little Amicalola Creek near the *Creek Trail* trailhead but nothing more.
Trail Time
A full loop of the park on the two ridge trails will take a hardy two hours; most canine hikers will opt for less.

12
Rabun
Bald

The Park

Rabun Bald tops out at 4,696 feet to place as runner-up for Georgia's highpoint, less than 100 feet shorter than Brasstown Bald to the west. Rabun's summit is not truly "bald" but covered with weather-beaten dwarf scarlet oak and evergreen rhododendron. The ridgeline that runs over Rabun Bald marks the Eastern Continental Divide - rainwater that falls on the north slope eventually drains into the Gulf of Mexico and water on the south slope will eventually wind up in the Atlantic Ocean via the Savannah River.

The Walks

The footpath to the top of Rabun Bald is along the 37-mile *Bartram Trail* that celebrates the work of 18th century botanist William Bartram. The access from Beegum Gap requires a 2.9-mile hike and a quicker ascent is found at the end of Kelsey Mountain Road where a short forest service trail links to the *Bartram Trail* and reaches the summit in 1.6 miles. You can also use an old road here as an alternate descent for half the canine hike.

Rabun County

Phone Number
- (706) 754-6221

Website
- fs.usda.gov/conf

Admission Fee
- None

Park Hours
- Sunrise to sunset

Directions
- *Chattahoochee National Forest*; northeast of Clayton. Take US 441 north and turn right onto GA 246 past Dillard. Continue into North Carolina onto NC106 and turn right onto Hale Ridge Road. At Bald Mountain Road turn right and go one mile to Kelsey Mountain Road and turn left. Park at the end. For Beegum Gap trailhead, stay on Hale Ridge Road at the junction which becomes Forest Service Road 7.

Your dog will travel through a rhododendron tunnel on his trip to the Rabun Bald summit.

This is an honest pull for your dog up Rabun Bald with nary a downhill step on the climb to the summit but never so severe as to bring even the less seasoned canine hiker to his knees. The final ascent utilizes lenghty switchbacks through thick stands of rhododendron, bent over by the weather on the exposed mountaintop. Your reward is a 360-degree, tri-state view that stretches for 100 miles on a clear day from the wooden observation deck.

The observation deck on Rabun Bald serves up 100-mile views of three states.

Trail Sense: The Forest Service trailhead is marked by a lime green blaze and wooden signs. The *Bartram Trail* is reliably lined with plastic yellow diamonds and it is the only trail to the summit.

Dog Friendliness
Dogs are welcome on the mountain.

Traffic
Foot travel only; parking is extremely limited at the trailhead so don't expect much competition on the path to the summit.

Canine Swimming
A few seeps near the summit is all.

Trail Time
Two to three hours.

13
John's Mountain

The Park

The Armuchee Unit - the name is believed to be a Cherokee derivation for "land of flowers" - is not packed with canine day hiking opportunities like the other ranger districts of the Chattahoochee National Forest and the twin trails of John's Mountain and Keown Falls are its prime attraction. The falls immortalize Marcus Gordon Keown, an educator at nearby Berry College that was founded as a girls' school by Martha Berry, who spent many years surveying the North Georgia woods.

Whitfield County

Phone Number
- (706) 695-6736

Website
- fs.usda.gov/conf

Admission Fee
- None

Park Hours
- Sunrise to sunset

Directions
- *Chattahoochee National Forest*; west of Resaca. From I-75 travel on GA 136 west. After about 14 miles turn left on Pocket County Road. Entrances to the recreation areas are between four and seven miles down Pocket Road.

The Walks

The two hiking loops of *John's Mountain* (3.5 miles) and *Keown Falls* (1.8 miles) link at the top of the falls where an observation deck lays open the eastern valley below. You can reach the grand junction from the John's Mountain Overlook above or the Keown Falls Scenic Area below. The *Keown Falls Loop* will present your dog with experiences not found elsewhere in the Atlanta area including a wide-ranging stone field (the stones have been gathered and laboriously placed to line the stem of the loop), a walk behind a waterfall (Keown Falls - there are two fed by small streams - can run dry and a trailhead sign will provide an update) and a cliffside walk under a seeping rockwall of water where fern gardens sprout. Although the trail gains about 500 feet in elevation the sharp switchbacks keep the grade modest enough for even the least experienced canine hiker. If you choose to continue onto the *Johns Mountain Loop* your dog will purchase views into Alabama and

Tennessee after bounding along the tops of the rock-edged mountainside.

Down the road south of Keown Falls is the Pocket Picnic Area where easy canine hiking awaits in a well-lubricated horseshoe-shaped valley framed by the Mill and Horn mountains. A 2.5-mile loop slips past sink holes that can be filled in the rainy season and support a vibrant wildflower community. If you are short on time

The Keown Falls Trail loops behind the waterfall as it spills over the cliff ledge.

the exploration can be shortened by sticking to the *Pocket Interpretive Nature Trail.*

Trail Sense: There are mapboards at the trailheads and it is a good idea to snap a picture with your smartphone. There are junction signs out on the trail that should keep you moving in the right direction.

Dog Friendliness
Dogs are welcome to hike these trails.
Traffic
Foot travel only.
Canine Swimming
The streams are only suitable for splashing and cooling off for your dog, even when they are flowing strong.
Trail Time
Two to three hours.

41

14
Reynolds
Nature Preserve

The Park

This land has a long legacy of farming although just how far back is uncertain since county records were burned in the Jonesboro courthouse during the Civil War. A barn built by Robert T.S. Huie, circa 1867, still stands and serves the park. In the 1920s a Clayton County judge, William Huie Reynolds purchased the then-decaying farm. Reynolds had taught himself the law and now applied the same initiatives to becoming a naturalist. For the next half-century he transformed the played-out fields into his own private nature preserve, delighting in showing off its wonders from behind the wheel of a Cadillac on what would become hiking trails generations later. In 1976 Judge Reynolds donated 130 acres to Clayton County as a green oasis in what is Georgia's third smallest county with the tenth most people.

Clayton County

Phone Number
- (770) 603-4188

Website
- reynoldsnaturepreserve.org

Admission Fee
- None

Park Hours
- 8AM-Dusk daily

Directions
- *Morrow*; 5665 Reynolds Road. Take Exit 233 off I-75, north on Jonesboro Road, Route 54. After 3/4 of a mile turn left on Reynolds Road and continue to the park on the left.

The highest point in Clayton County is in the park.

The Walks

The four-mile trail system at Reynolds Nature Preserve is a knitted quiltwork of stacked loops from which many types of canine hikes can be derived. The *Perimeter Trail* covers 1.5 miles and touches most of the park's attractions which include historic structures, ponds that Judge Reynolds constructed from several springs on the property and a climb to the highest elevation in the park, and Clayton County, at 1,116-foot Back Mountain. The ponds and Back Mountain can each be reached on their own one-mile loop trails - the latter on the *Burstin' Heart Trail* which, despite its ominous name, will only set your dog to panting for a short spell. Side trails abound,

including a boardwalk trail and short detours to hidden ponds and swamps. These are wooded rambles through a predominantly hardwood forest sprinkled with pines on beautifully formed natural footpaths.

Trail Sense: A mapboard with trail descriptions is at the parking lot and a trail map can be downloaded from the website. Signs are posted at trail junctions to point the way.

Dog Friendliness
Dogs are welcome to trot these peaceful trails.

Traffic
Foot traffic only.

Canine Swimming
The wetland ponds in the Nature Preserve are best enjoyed by the frogs and turtles.

Trail Time
You can craft any type of canine hike your dog desires at Reynolds Nature Preserve from short, easy strolling to a brisk trail workout.

15
Dawson Forest Wildlife Management Area

The Park

There are over 28,000 acres in the Dawson Forest Wildlife Management Area and the best canine hiking is right on the main road - no long, bumpy drives into the wilderness required. Work on the trail has been done by the Mountain Stewards, a group of Southern Appalachian Mountain hikers who banded together in 2003 and have spruced up and built over 30 miles of trails since.

The Walks

The three-mile *Amicalola River Trail* is one of the best single destination trails you can hike with your dog in the Atlanta region. After an initial half-mile handicap-accessible stroll

Dawson County

Phone Number
- None

Website
- mountainstewards.org

Admission Fee
- User fee

Park Hours
- Sunrise to sunset

Directions
- *Dawsonville*; west of town. Take GA 53 west to the parking area on the right just before the road crosses the Amicacola River. The trail is on the opposite side of GA 53, accessed from under the bridge.

along the river the trail becomes a footpath and turns away from the river as it climbs into the surrounding hillside. The roar of the river, which was ever-present on the first stage of the hike fades into the crevasses of the hillsides. Your dog will be trotting on a sweeping rollercoaster as the path works its way up to the piney ridges pn the highest point in the area, where a memorial honors Jason Funk, whose Eagle Scout project was this trail before he passed away at the age of 16. The *Amicalola River Trail* was imagined as an interpretive trail but today about half the signs have either been destroyed or refer to landmarks that are no longer there. After cresting the ridge the final mile is as sweet a stretch of canine hiking as you are likely to find - a wide, pine-draped descent to the Amicalola River.

The churning "Edge of the World" rapids provide the visual excitement along the Amicalola River Trail.

Trail Sense: There are no maps but the trail is well-blazed, including one critical left-turn off a forest-service road about two miles in.

Dog Friendliness
Dogs are allowed to hike on the *Amicalola River Trail*.

Traffic
Foot travel only and considerably less of it once the waterside boardwalk trail ends.

Canine Swimming
When the water is down and the river is passably tame there will be plenty of dogs enjoying canine aquatics here.

Trail Time
Between one and two hours.

16
Unicoi
State Park

The Park

This area was known as the "Land of 1,000 Waterfalls" to the Cherokee Nation that lived here for hundreds of years. After the Cherokee were driven out in the early 1800s, the land was ridden hard by incoming settlers who first arrived in pursuit of gold. "Gold Fever" lasted but a short time in Georgia but here hydraulic mining operations - a destructive practice eventually outlawed - stripped the land. Around the turn of the 20th century the Byrd-Matthews Lumber Company bought most it and began toppling trees that were hauled down to Helen (the town was named for the daughter of a timber executive) on a narrow gauge railroad and milled. Soon nearly 70,000 board feet of lumber was shipping out of Helen every day. By the 1930s the hillside was bare and the sawmill shuttered. The government began to buy up the scarred land and organize the Chattahoochee National Forest that included the 1,600-acre Anna Ruby Falls Scenic Area and the 1,050-acre Unicoi State Park.

White County

Phone Number
- (706) 878-2201

Website
- gastateparks.org/Unicoi

Admission Fee
- $5 parking fee

Park Hours
- 7 AM - 10 PM daily

Directions
- *Helen*; two miles northeast of town. Take GA 17/75 north and make the first right onto GA 356 to the park entrances on the left.

The Walks

The star walk at Unicoi State Park is the 2.5-mile *Lake Loop* that circles the 53-acre Unicoi Lake. Save for a stretch on the east shore this gently rolling loop hugs the water most of the way and serves up picturesque vistas of knobby mountains that ring the lake. Note: to close the loop you will have to do a short bit of roadway-walking with your dog across the dam.

Canine hikers seeking more of a challenge can tackle the 4.8-mile *Smith Creek Trail* that starts at the campground and ends at the spectacular headwaters of Smith Creek where the twin waterfalls known as Anna Ruby Falls tumble off Tray Mountain. Fed by underground springs, Curtis Creek falls 153 feet in a double drop and York Creek concludes its run with a 50-foot plunge. Anna Ruby Falls is administered by the USDA Forest Service and can also be reached by car and a paved, uphill .4-mile hike (a separate admission

The headwaters of Smith Creek are formed by Anna Ruby Falls, a rare double waterfall.

fee is required for vehicular entrance). You can return to Unicoi State Park back down the *Smith Creek Trail* or close the loop by hiking on paved park roads.

In the other direction, another one-way trail runs three miles to the town of Helen, Georgia's third largest tourist destination. If you are staying in Helen you can hike with your dog to the park from Unicoi Hill City Park.

Trail Sense: A superb color map is available at the Visitor Center.

Dog Friendliness
Dogs allowed on the trail and in the campground. Dogs are not allowed on the small lake beach, which the *Lake Loop Trail* crosses, during the active season.

Traffic
There is a separate mountain bike trail in the park.

Canine Swimming
There are a few places where your dog can slip into Unicoi Lake for some canine swimming.

Trail Time
Several hours to a full day available surrounding Unicoi State Park.

17
Crockford-Pigeon Mountain WMA

The Park

Pigeon Mountain stretches ten miles roughly northeast to southwest and took its name from the enormous roosts of passenger pigeons that once lived here. There were an estimated five billion wild pigeons in the United States when the Europeans arrived in North America but they were blasted into extinction by 1914. More than 16,000 acres of the mountain have been under the management of the Georgia Department of Natural Resources since 1969.

The Walks

You can take some of your longest, most solitary hikes with your dog on Pigeon Mountain, most notably on the blue-blazed *Pocket Loop*. The trail picks up about 1,400 feet in elevation in the course of its ten miles and is highlighted by geological formations and the tumbling waters of Pocket Creek Falls. There is extended hiking along the ridgeline once you get there. The Pocket is justly hailed as one of Georgia's best wildflower hunting spots, which is traversed by a boardwalk near the head of the trail.

Walker County

Phone Number
- (706) 295-6041

Website
- n-georgia.com/wildlife.htm

Admission Fee
- daily use fee

Park Hours
- Sunrise to sunset

Directions
- *LaFayette*; west of town. Take GA 193 west 2.7 miles to Chamberlain Road and turn left. Go 3 miles to Rocky Lane Road and turn right. The check station will be on your left.

The "Champagne Glass" is one of the fanciful formations your dog will discover in Rocktown.

The most popular trail on Pigeon Mountain is one of the easiest for your dog in North Georgia, the mile-long trot on a wide, sandy path to the jumble of massive boulders known as Rocktown. Covering some 150 acres, these eroded sandstone formations in-deed look like weathered building foundation ruins in places. Other jumbled

boulders will trigger your imagination for descriptive adjectives and you can only imagine what your dog is thinking as she bounds in and out and up and down the inhabitants of Rocktown.

Trail Sense: The trails are blazed and a superb map can be picked up at the check station.

Dog Friendliness
Dogs are welcome in the Wildlife Management Area, which includes a dog training area.

Traffic
Most of the trails and roads are multi-use but the Rocktown Trail is hiker-only.

Canine Swimming
This will be a hiking adventure for your dog rather than a swimming event.

Trail Time
A full day possible.

18
Burnt Mountain Preserve

The Park

After the Cherokees were rudely dispatched in the early 1830s, Scotch-Irish from the Carolinas made their way to Georgia to settle in the southernmost mountains of the Appalachians. They raised what they needed to survive but the soil on the 3,000-foot mountains was thin and the growing season short. Nevertheless, by the Civil War Burnt Mountain Community boasted a church, a school, a grist mill and the mark of existence - a post office.

This mountain, which has two peaks, was also known as Burrell Top since the brothers Joseph and Grandville lived here. But the future lay in the developing valleys not on the mountaintops so the Burrells sold out to George Marble tycoon Sam Tate and moved to Alabama to raise cotton. Tate had grand plans to develop the "prettiest town on a mountain in the South" with a lodge, a golf course, and an airfield all designed by the leading architects of the day. Connahaynee Lodge opened on Burnt Mountain peak but the Great Depression lurked around the corner. Tate Mountain Estates filed for bankruptcy in 1934 and the lodge burned to the ground in March of 1946. There has been no further development on the mountain for three-quarters of a century and the trail system on Burnt Mountain, now owned by Pickens County, was built in 2006 by the Mountain Stewards, a private advocacy group.

Pickens County

Phone Number
- None

Website
- mountainstewards.org

Admission Fee
- None

Park Hours
- Sunrise to sunset

Directions
- *Jasper*, northeast of town. From GA 53 in the center of town take Burnt Mountain Road north out of town until it joins GA 136 in three miles. Bear right and continue east another three miles to the parking area on the right.

The Walks

The canine hiking on Burnt Mountain comes from three stacked loops that with satisfy any level of trail dog. You will start out at an elevation of 2,500 feet and how far you drop off the mountain will determine your dog's hiking day. The log-lined trails travel through stands of second-growth hardwoods (most of the trees were cleared for the Connahaynee Lodge) with little understory so during the winter months there are impressive south-facing vistas. The *Crest Trail* stubbornly defies sliding down the

Your dog will earn any rest he takes on Burnt Mountain.

hillsides and will be completed in an easy 15 minutes by any canine hiker. The yellow-blazed *Preserve Trail* winds 400 feet down Burnt Mountain but just before it appears you are on a never-ending descent it makes a sharp left-turn to return to the mountaintop after a mile. These are just warm-ups for athletic dogs to bound a full 800 feet down into Champion Creek Valley. There are some switchbacks cut into the two-mile *Champion Creek Trail* but this hike will set any dog to panting.

Trail Sense: No maps but well-blazed and signed trails.

Dog Friendliness
Dogs are welcome on the mountain.

Traffic
Foot travel only; no bikes.

Canine Swimming
A few streams trickle down the mountain but this is a place for dog hiking; deep explorations of Champion Creek reveal waterfalls and plunge pools.

Trail Time
From 30 to 90 minutes, typically.

19
Chattahoochee Bend State Park

The Park

When Chattahoochee Bend State Park opened in the summer of 2011, after two years of construction, it was the first new state park opened by the Georgia Department of Natural Resources in almost two decades. With 2,910 acres of wilderness - including five miles of river frontage - only three state parks in the system are larger. Twelve chunks of land, most significantly a 560-acre donation from the Georgia Power Company, were cobbled together to create the park which has been left mostly in its natural state.

The Walks

The nascent trail system in Georgia's newest state park is still evolving but the star trail that traces the river for the better part of five miles has opened. The *Riverside Trail* doesn't hug the shoreline but the lazy water is never more than a few leaps away. Your dog will be trotting mostly on paw-friendly sandy loam as the path alternates between flat stretches and gentle ups-and-downs. Under a canopy of yawning hardwoods, the trail reaches the namesake bend in the Chattahoochee. Once here, the route pushes away from the river and pitches and rolls with more conviction.

Coweta County

Phone Number
- (770) 254-7271

Website
- gastateparks.org/ChattahoocheeBend

Admission Fee
- $5 parking fee

Park Hours
- 7 AM - 10 PM

Directions
- *Newnan*; 425 Bobwhite Way. From I-85 North or South near Newnan, take Exit 47 off GA 34 (Bullsboro Blvd.). Go west .8 miles. Turn right onto Highway 34 Bypass (M Farmer Industrial Blvd.) and go 6 miles. Turn right onto GA 34 (Franklin Road) at 4-way stop and go 8.2 miles. Turn right onto Thomas Powers Road and go 2.7 miles to a 4-way stop. The road name changes to Hewlett South Road. Continue straight .9 miles. Bear left onto Bud Davis Road and go 1.9 miles. Turn right onto Flat Rock Road. The road name changes to Bobwhite Way. Continue straight to gated entrance of the park.

Your dog can easily access views of the Chattahoochee River and surrounding forestscape from the park's two-story observation tower.

An *East-West Trail* has been cut from the Visitor Center to the Chattahoochee River that reveals more of the undulating flavor of the park as it travels through grasses and pines. Park roads can be used to create loops but for the most part canine hiking here will be an out-and-back affair.

Trail Sense: A line drawing park map is available.

Dog Friendliness
Dogs are allowed on the park trails and in the campground.

Traffic
Foot traffic only on the trails.

Canine Swimming
Access to the Chattahoochee River from the trail is problematic with its high banks - the best place for a doggie dip is at the boat ramp in the picnic area.

Trail Time
More than an hour.

20
Springer Mountain

The Park

In 1958 Springer Mountain went from being one of many non-descript, anonymous 3,000-foot peaks in the North Georgia to being world famous when it was designated the southern terminus of the *Appalachian Trail*. At the time many people didn't even call it Springer Mountain, it was also known as Penitentiary Mountain. No one is sure why, just as the origins of the name Springer Mountain are lost to the vapors of history, although there were Springers of some prominence who settled in the area in the early 1800s.

From the time the *Appalachian Trail* was completed in 1937 the terminus had been at Mount Oglethorpe, the southernmost peak in the Blue Ridge Mountains and the highest peak in Pickens County. The construction of a gravel logging road and the build-up of chicken farms on the mountain led to the relocation of the jumping off point for the celebrated trail. The idea for a footpath up the spine of the Appalachian Mountains was hatched by Benton MacKaye, a forester, in 1921. MacKaye wanted to provide an epic trail that would link farms and wilderness camps for the benefit of city-dwellers. Construction began in New York in 1923 and today the *Appalachian Trail* runs through 14 states for more than 2,100 miles (75 in Georgia) after leaving Springer Mountain. The trail is within a day's drive of 200 million people.

Gilmer County

Phone Number
- (706) 754-6221

Website
- fs.usda.gov/conf

Admission Fee
- None

Park Hours
- Sunrise to sunset

Directions
- *Chattahoochee National Forest*; west of Dahlonega. Take GA 52 west for 9 miles and turn right at an old store towards Nimblewill Baptist Church. After two miles turn right on Forest Service Road 28-1 (if you reach the church, you've gone too far.) When the gravel road forks, go up to the left on Forest Service Road 77. After 5 miles turn left on Forest Service Road 42 and continue to the parking lot on the right. There are brown Forest Service signs to help you along.

The Walks

Multi-day hikers favor the approach to Springer Mountain from 8.5 miles away in Amicacola Falls State Park but the quickest way to the southern terminus is from a parking lot in the Chattahoochee National Forest.

Here you will actually be starting with your dog .9 of a mile into the *Appalachian Trail* and be hiking back south to the terminus on top of the summit. The climb is a gradual one along the rocky side of the mountain with long-ranging views of the surrounding highlands.

If your goal is just to see the terminus a return down the mountain completes your dog's day on Springer Mountain. But extended canine hiking is possible by looping back about six miles on the *Benton MacKaye Trail* that joins the *Appalachian Trail* just below the summit where it launches a 300-mile journey of its own to Tennessee.

This is the touchstone for hikers starting or, less frequently, finishing the six-month journey on the Appalachian Trail.

Trail Sense: The *Appalachian Trail* is marked by iconic white blazes; spur trails are blazed in blue. The *MacKaye Trail* uses white diamonds.

Dog Friendliness
Dogs are welcome along these long-distance footpaths.

Traffic
The trail can get crowded, especially in the early spring when thru-hikers start to gather.

Canine Swimming
There are no streams between the forest road and the summit but small streams are crossed further north and on the *MacKaye-Appalachian* loop.

Trail Time
Anywhere from an hour to six months.

21
Tallulah Gorge State Park

The Park

In 1882 the Tallulah Falls Railway was constructed to bring tourists to the three-mile gorge named for the Choctaw word for "leaping water." Guest houses sprung up along the rims of the 1,000-foot crack caused by the Tallulah River cutting through the Tallulah Dome rock formation. Buggies and horses conveyed gawkers to the series of falls known collectively as Tallulah Falls.

In 1913 a hydroelectric dam built by Georgia Railway and Power to run Atlanta's streetcars virtually eliminated the falls and eight years later a fire wiped out the town and its hospitality infrastructure. For most of the remainder of the 20th century the gorge was managed primarily as a utility, although Hollywood came calling in 1971 to film the scene in *Deliverance* when Jon Voight climbed out of the canyon. Although Confederate General James Longstreet's widow, Helen, lobbied to make the gorge a state park in 1911, it was not until 1993 that Tallulah Gorge State Park was created, restoring the river's recreational mojo.

Habersham County

Phone Number
- (706) 754-7981

Website
- gastateparks.org/TallulahGorge

Admission Fee
- $5 parking fee

Park Hours
- 7 AM - 10 PM daily

Directions
- *Tallulah Falls*; in town on either side of US 441, north of Tallulah Gorge.

The Walks

Your dog's adventure in the "Niagara of the South" is severely curtailed by a ban on canine hiking beneath the gorge rims so a tourist experience is more in the offing here. The park features rim trails of a little less than a mile on either side, connecting by the highway crossing the dam. The short section of the *North Rim Trail* on either side of the Interpretive Center is covered in wood chips and pulverized tires (we are told 60 of them were eliminated from the waste system for the walking path) leads to three viewpoints that capture the essence of Tallulah Gorge. The full exploration covers about three miles of canine hiking on natural, slightly inclined trails and entail ten viewpoints. The only spot of possible bother for your dog is the 212-foot climb in 1/4-mile to Inspiration Point. Although the park sign warns of an unfinished trail and unprotected cliff edges, neither is true. Beyond Inspiration Point is an old road that leads into the park wilderness, the *Stoneplace Trail*, that can be explored by permit.

Trail Sense: Not a problem.

The tower that anchored the wire used by Karl Wallenda to cross Tallulah Gorge in 1971, built at a cost of $50,000, remains in the park.

Dog Friendliness

Dogs are not allowed below the gorge rim or on the gorge floor. Dogs are also not permitted on the beach above the dam.

Traffic

Foot traffic only and heavy around the Interpretive Center; mountain bikes can use the *Stoneplace Trail*.

Canine Swimming

Down-sloping streams cross the *North Rim Trail*; not deep enough for swimming but do offer a cool splash on a hot day.

Trail Time

About two hours to fully explore the Tallulah Gorge rims.

22
Autrey Mill
Nature Preserve

The Park

The history of this land is a familiar Georgia tale: Creek Indians living in small villages were pushed out by the Cherokee who were forced out by the Americans. The lush forests around the watershed were cleared for cash crops, mostly cotton but some corn and wheat as well. But the story ends differently - instead of winding up as suburban housing a grassroots effort by community activists rescued the property to create the 46-acre Nature Preserve that is flavored with historic buildings reflecting 400 years of history here.

The Walks

The trail system at Autrey Mill packs over two miles of canine hiking into its compact property. The trails flow down a hillside towards Sal's Creek where the five-story Autrey Mill operated back at the end of the 1800s. Pieces of the stone dam and foundation are about all that can be seen of the mill today along the *River Trail*. This is easy going for your dog on pine straw-strewn natural paths with plenty of wooden bridges to carry you over the rough spots.

Fulton County

Phone Number
- (678) 366-3511

Website
- autreymill.org

Admission Fee
- None

Park Hours
- Grounds open during daylight hours

Directions
- *Johns Creek*; 9770 Autrey Mill Road. From Route I-285 take Exit 31 north on Peachtree Indsutrial Boulevard, Route 141. Bear left on 141 as it becomes Peachtree Parkway NW and, after it crosses the Chattahoochee River, Medlock Bridge Road. After the river turn left on Old Alabama Road and continue to the park on the right.

The mysterious monkeys of Autrey Mill.

Take some time to tour the Heritage Village with its Native American dwellings and restored buildings such as the 1880s Summerour House. And on the *Forest Trail* stop and consider the concrete monkeys. Many years ago a circus train wrecked on the tracks near Duluth, freeing all the animals. The monkeys stuck together and fled en masse to the woods near the Summerour House. The farmers, having never seen a monkey, blasted the alien creatures out of the trees until every last simian fugitive was dead. Never let the facts get in the way of a good story when you are hiking with your dog.

Trail Sense: Trail maps are available in the Visitor Center and signposts mark the trails.

Dog Friendliness
Dogs are allowed on the trails in the Nature Preserve.

Traffic
Foot traffic only.

Canine Swimming
Sal's Creek is a lively ribbon of water but there are pools where your dog can get in and paddle around.

Trail Time
Less than one hour.

23
Allatoona Pass Battlefield

The Park

The State of Georgia chartered the Western & Atlantic Railroad in 1837 and it took 13 years to finish a twisting, 137-mile route through the mountains to Chattanooga, Tennessee. A chunk of that time was spent here, blasting a 360-foot long, 175-foot deep cut through solid rock, the deepest rail cut along the entire Western & Atlantic line. The railroad became critical as a supply line to Atlanta during the Civil War. First, in 1862, non-uniformed Union soldiers led by James Andrews commandeered a Confederate locomotive, "The General," at Big Shanty, 13 miles to the south and headed north, furiously shoveling coal and attempting to damage the tracks behind it. The raiders made it through the Pass but "The Great Locomotive Chase" ended before the spies could get out of Georgia. Andrews and seven co-cospirators were hanged but some of his men were awarded the nation's first Congressional Medals of Honor.

After the fall of Atlanta, the Allatoona Pass had changed hands and was fortified by General William T. Sherman. In October of 1864 it was

Bartow County

Phone Number
- None

Website
- evhsonline.org/allatoona/

Admission Fee
- None

Park Hours
- Sunrise to sunset

Directions
- *Emerson*; east of town. From I-75 take Exit 283 to the east. After 1.5 miles, when the road bends right, turn left into the second entrance of the small parking lot at the levee for Lake Allatoona.

Canine hiking at Allatoona Pass travels through the historic railroad cut.

the Confederates' turn to attack the Federal supply lines. Only the arrival of reinforcements kept the Pass in Union hands but the fighting here was some of the most hotly contested of the Civil War with casualty rates over 35%. The railroad stopped

Lakeside monuments remember the small, but bloody, Civil War action at Allatoona Pass.

running in the 1940s and most of the battlefield became the property of the U.S. Army Corps of Engineers which became Lake Allatoona.

The Walks

Save for the re-forested hills the topography of Allatoona Pass remains much the same today as it did when Civil War armies clashed here. Even the Clayton/Mooney house across from the parking lot as you start down the trail is still in its place, complete with bullet holes. Your dog will trot easily down the old roadbed of the historic Western & Atlantic Railroad through the Deep Cut. Side trips up the adjoining slopes will uncover traces of earthen forts that once guarded the Pass. Wooden stairways will help your dog negotiate the high spots.

Trail Sense: Interpretive signs will lead you around the battlefield. There is no "proper" way to visit the sites so don't be concerned with the order you encounter history here.

Dog Friendliness
Dogs are welcome to explore the battlefield.
Traffic
Foot travel only.
Canine Swimming
Lake Allatoona stands ready to host a doggie dip.
Trail Time
Up to an hour or more, depending how deeply you immerse your dog in Civil War history.

24
Stone Mountain Park

The Park

Like a land iceberg, the massive exposed dome of Stone Mountain is only the tip of a slab of granite that extends nine miles underground. With a high point of 1,683 feet rising 780 feet above the surrounding countryside it is the largest of many exposed granite plutons in Georgia and one of the largest exposed granite domes in America.

Stone Mountain has been a recreational destination since the early 1800s and promoter Aaron Cloud erected a 165-foot wooden observation tower on the summit in 1838, reached by a 1.1- mile mountaintop trail similar to the one today. The mountain was quarried from the 1830s and privately owned after 1887 for excavation. The State of Georgia purchased Stone Mountain in 1958 for $1,125,000 and has since developed over 3,000 acres as a family vacation destination.

DeKalb County
Phone Number - (770) 498-5690
Website - stonemountainpark.com
Admission Fee - $10 parking fee
Park Hours - 6 AM - Midnight daily
Directions - *Stone Mountain Park*; 15 miles east of downtown Atlanta on US Highway 78. Take exit 39 B off I-285 and follow Highway 78 east for 8 miles. The main entrance for Stone Mountain Park is Exit 8 that funnels directly into the park.

The Walks

Dogs cannot go for the glory by trotting on the *Walk-Up Trail* to the summit of Stone Mountain but can visit most of the other attractions in the park on the *Cherokee Trail* that makes a five-mile circumference of the granite monadnock. These include lakes, views of the mountain, a grist mill, a quarry exhibit and a covered bridge that spanned the Oconee River in Athens until 1965. When it was slated for demolition the park purchased the wooden bridge for a dollar and reassembled it here. This is easy going for your dog most of the way but since the *Cherokee Trail* crosses a sliver of the mountain where dogs are banned you will have to improvise on a connector trail to complete the loop.

For dogs that aren't up for a full tour of Stone Mountain the *Nature Garden Trail* trips along a scenic 3/4 mile loop trail through a mature oak-hickory forest while highlighting native Georgia plants.

Trail Sense: A park map comes with admission and maps for the individual trails can be pulled off the website.

Dog Friendliness

Dogs are not allowed anywhere on Stone Mountain or in the Songbird Habitat Trail Area.

Traffic

This is the place to come for a communal dog walk.

Canine Swimming

The necklace of lakes on the southern and eastern ends of the mountain are alluring but not easily accessible.

Trail Time

The short nature trail can be experienced in less than a half-hour; the *Cherokee Trail* around the base will require the better part of two hours.

25
Smithgall Woods
State Park

The Park

Charles A. Smithgall, Jr., the son of a Florida lumberman, walked into the studios of WGST, the radio station at Georgia Tech, in the early 1930s and landed a job as a student announcer. Smithgall would go on to found the *Gainesville Times* and own radio and television stations in north Georgia and Alabama. A fervent conservationist Smithgall assembled 5,500 acres of land along Duke's Creek from 1983 to 1994 through 81 individual land transactions. He then sold the property for 50¢ on the dollar to the State of Georgia as a gift-purchase.

> ### White County
>
> **Phone Number**
> - (706) 878-3087
>
> **Website**
> - gastateparks.org/SmithgallWoods
>
> **Admission Fee**
> - $5 parking fee except on Wednesdays
>
> **Park Hours**
> - 7 AM - 10 PM daily
>
> **Directions**
> - *Helen*; three miles west of town on GA 75 Alternate.

Georgia's Gold Rush of 1829 started with a nugget pulled out of a tributary of Duke's Creek but today the trout, mostly wily natives, are the prize in the water. Its status as North Georgia's premier trout stream forces the park to limit the number of anglers here.

The Walks

The canine hiking in the conservation area is really a series of short spurts that branch off the paved *Tsalaki Trail* from the Visitor Center to about three miles down Duke's Creek. The *Laurel Ridge Interpretive Trail* and the *Wetlands Loop Trail* each examine the natural gifts of open fields, lush woods and beaver ponds. *Martin's Mine Trail* visits the Gold Rush days to see shafts dug into the hillsides and century-old mining debris. The final exploration is along the *Cathy Ellis Memorial Trail* where the first gold nugget was pulled from the creek by a local slavehand. Today the stream's go-to attraction is a cascading waterfall.

The primo walk at Duke's Creek is just outside the park, however, in the Dukes Creek Falls Recreation Area, administered by the Chattahoochee National Forest (two miles down the Russell Scenic Highway off GA 75 Alternate). Here a wide, beautifully engineered trail lowers canine hikers 400 feet over the course of a switchbacking mile to where the falls of Davis Creek and the lively cascades of Dukes Creek mingle uproariously below an observation deck.

Trail Sense: Once you identify where each trail is, you won't get lost on them.

Davis Creek makes a spectacular - and loud - entrance into Dukes Creek.

Dog Friendliness
Dogs are allowed to hike along Duke's Creek.

Traffic
Foot traffic and shuttle buses; bikes are allowed to use the dozen or so miles of road trails in Smithgall Woods.

Canine Swimming
As long as your dog doesn't scare the fish.

Trail Time
You can complete a canine hike in less than an hour or spend most of the day doing them all.

26
Oconee Heritage Park

The Park

Oconee County created this 364-acre park to host agricultural-themed events in a large open air arena, including rodeos and dog shows. But there is no need for your dog to sit on the sidelines at Heritage Park because behind the arena are...

The Walks

...more than a dozen miles of wooded trails. There are no grand destinations here - just hours of hiking with your dog. The paths have been created for bikes and horses but are open to canine hikers as well. The newer of the two, the *Equestrian Trail*, essentially loops the property in a five-mile journey. Your dog will find more room to stretch out here as the trail is generally four to six feet wide as opposed to the serpentine *Bike Trail* where the narrow single track folds back on itself often as it winds up slopes and around gullies. Expect a stream crossing or two and once your dog plunges into the woodlands you will be inside the young, airy forest the entire hike.

Trail Sense: A map is available for downloading on the website and unless you come with a mission to explore, bring the map because it can get disorienting in the featureless woods.

Oconee County

Phone Number
- (706) 769-3965

Website
- ocprd.com/heritage-park.aspx

Admission Fee
- None

Park Hours
- Sunrise to sunset

Directions
- *Watkinsville*; 2543 Macon Highway. From I-20 take Exit 114 north on Route 441 through Madison. Stay on 441 (there are many route numbers that share the road) until you reach the park on the left, 10 miles north of town.

The open space in front of this rustic cabin is a great spot for a game of fetch - behind it the canine hiking is all in the woods.

Dog Friendliness

Dogs are allowed to trot these trails.

Traffic

More bikes than horses make the equestrian trail the better choice, especially on a warm weekend.

Canine Swimming

This is a park for canine hikers, not canine swimmers.

Trail Time

You can craft a canine hike of any duration from a half-hour hour to several hours.

27
Clinton
Nature Preserve

The Park

Joseph Carnes, whose Scotch-Irish ancestors settled in New England in the 1680s, was born in Frederick County, Maryland in 1753. After serving as a private in the Virginia Militia during the American Revolution Carnes married Comfort Ann Cash in 1783 and migrated south into North Carolina where a son, John Thomas, was born. By the early 1800s the family was in Georgia and prior to 1830 the Carnes clan was settled here where Comfort was one of the fourteen charter members of the New Hope Primitive Baptist Church. In 1832 John Carnes purchased this property for $200 from Elizabeth Farmer who pulled a lucky number in a Georgia land lottery. The farm passed through four family generations until 200 acres was donated to Douglas County by Annie Mae Clinton in 1983 with the provision that the park remain in its natural state.

Douglas County

Phone Number
- (770) 920-7129

Website
- celebratedouglascounty.com

Admission Fee
- None

Park Hours
- Daily, sunrise to sunset

Directions
- *Villa Rica*; 8720 Ephesus Church Road. From I-20 take Exit 30 south on the Post Road for a half-mile to Ephesus Church Road on the right. Follow Ephesus Church for a mile to the park entrance on the right.

The Walks

There are a trio of hiking loops here - four if you include the half-mile walking trail - that will suit any level of canine hiker. The *Blue Trail* is the easiest ramble in the park, a stand-alone affair of nearly a mile. The *Yellow and Red Trails* intertwine, mixing old farm roads and narrow, twisting footpaths along the way. Footing under paw can be tricky off the wide roads with exposed roots, stony patches and even remnants of old asphalt. The full trip on the *Red Trail* will cover over four miles and serve up a full exploration of

Several outbuildings and structures dating as far back as the 1830s can be stumbled upon during a canine hike in the Clinton Nature Preserve.

the Nature Preserve. The canine hike gets progressively hillier and traverses increasingly rougher terrain that will test even the most athletic dog before you are done.

Trail Sense: A park map is available and will come in handy when navigating the power lines that dissect the property. The color-coded trails are reliably blazed.

Dog Friendliness
Dogs are allowed on the park trails.
Traffic
Foot traffic only on the trails.
Canine Swimming
The farm lake will be your water-loving dog's first stop at Clinton Nature Preserve.
Trail Time
More than an hour.

28
Chattahoochee River NRA-Jones Bridge

The Park

Jones Bridge was built here in 1904 to replace a ferry operation across the Chattahoochee River. By the 1930s the bridge's oak roadbed was decaying and Fulton County and Gwinnett County squabbled over who should pay for repairs. So the bridge was closed down. In the 1940s a crew showed up and began dismantling the bridge. They hauled away half the bridge for scrap before anyone realized the work was never authorized. The remainder of Jones Bridge and its piers still stand in the Chattahoochee.

The Walks

Canine hiking here rolls out south of Jones Bridge, closely tracing the Chattahoochee River on a single band until the trail system breaks into a spiderweb of short segments. Athletic dogs will want to test the climbs to the low ridges but you can just as easily keep your entire hike at Jones Bridge with scarcely an uphill step. If you veer away from the river your dog will find five or so miles of rambling in the oak-beech hardwood forest that is punctuated by rhododendron and magnolia.

Trail Sense: There are mapboards on site and even a wrong turn or two will never leave you far from the river.

Fulton County

Phone Number
- (678) 538-1200

Website
- nps.gov/chat

Admission Fee
- Parking fee

Park Hours
- Sunrise to sunset

Directions
- *Roswell*; east of town. From GA 400, take Exit 7A, and travel east 4.1 miles and turn left on Barnwell Road. Go two miles to Jones Bridge on the right (past the Environmental Center entrance). Descend the entrance road, going past the boat trailer lot to the main parking area.

This was a crime scene in the 1940s when crews illegally dismantled half of Jones Bridge and hauled it away for scrap.

Dog Friendliness

Dogs can hike these trails and poop bags are provided.

Traffic

Foot traffic only.

Canine Swimming

The boat ramp and canoe launches provide the best access for your dog into the river where it flows over rocky shoals as it passes.

Trail Time

Anything from a quick leg stretcher to a two-hour canine hike is possible at Jones Bridge.

29
McDaniel Farm Park

The Park

This land came into the McDaniel family in 1859 when Eli McDaniel plunked down $450 on the Gwinnett County Courthouse steps for 125 acres of Georgia woods. Eli began carving a farm that would be maintained in the family all the way until 1999. This was subsistence farming with practically everything the McDaniels needed coming from the land. Electricity did not arrive until the 1950s when mules were still plowing the fields. When Archie McDaniel died at the age of 78, after 66 years of caring for the farm, Gwinnett County purchased the property to create a recreational and educational showcase.

Gwinnett County

Phone Number
- (770) 814-4920

Website
- gwinnettcounty.com

Admission Fee
- None

Park Hours
- 7 AM - dusk daily

Directions
- *Duluth*; 3251 McDaniel Road. Take Exit 104 off I-85 north on Pleasant Hill Road. Turn right on Satellite Boulevard, left on Old Norcross Road and right on McDaniel Road into the park.

The Walks

Although you are literally in the shadow of Gwinnett Place Mall and platoons of other shopping centers and traffic snarls while on the trail in McDaniel Farm Park your dog will never know it. After you drop down the long hill behind the farm the paved path rolls through open fields and sparse woodlands oblivious to the suburban cacophony that surrounds it.

The nearly three miles of multi-use paths are paved but there are opportunities for your dog to trot alongside on natural grass. And unlike most Atlanta trails that spend their time under a leafy canopy, McDaniel Farm is a great place to soak up the rays as you hike with your dog on a sunny day. Some of the meadows were never grazed or plowed and the double-loop trail trips through a perpetual wildflower habitat. And what would a farm

**McDaniel Farm gives your trail dog a chance
to connect with his inner farm dog.**

be without an open field for a game of fetch? You can find it here.

Trail Sense: There is a large mapboard and "You Are Here" maps at the trail junctions in the double loop making it nigh impossible to get lost.

Dog Friendliness

Dogs are allowed on the trails and poop bag containers are usually filled by park users.

Traffic

You can encounter bikes and skaters on the paved paths but expect far more pedestrians and dog walkers.

Canine Swimming

The creek that slices through the loop trail is not deep enough for swimming but provides a perfect splash for cooling off on a hot day.

Trail Time

About one hour.

30
Chattahoochee River NRA-Vickery Creek

The Park

Roswell King was a plantation manager on the Georgia coast who migrated here in 1836 and began construction of a four-story cotton mill powered by the cascading waters of Vickery Creek. By the outbreak of the Civil War there were six structures on the property and a town around the factory. Vickery Creek looms cranked out the "Roswell Gray" fabric that was sewed into Confederate military uniforms.

When Union General William T. Sherman embarked on his Atlanta Campaign the Roswell Mills became a military target. On July 5, 1864 Union troops seized the mill and the 400 workers, nearly all women and children, were arrested and charged with treason. They were held in Marietta before many were placed on over-crowded rail cars and deported to the North, igniting an outcry in both the Northern and Southern newspapers. Only a handful would ever return to their Georgia homes. The mills at Roswell were rebuilt after the War and continued to operate until 1975. Now the historic site is administered by the National Park Service.

Fulton County

Phone Number
- (678) 538-1200

Website
- nps.gov/chat

Admission Fee
- Parking fee

Park Hours
- Sunrise to sunset

Directions
- *Roswell*; several access points, including Mill Street in town. Vickery Creek enters the Chattahoochee River at the junction of Riverside Road and Roswell Road (Route 9).

The Walks

Most of the canine hiking in this Unit of the Chattahoochee River NRA takes place on the easy rolls of a wooded knob above the twisting gorge that has been carved by Vickery Creek. If you start at the Riverside Road lot and come from 300 feet below to the ridge, take heed of the trail closures on the rocky shore and do not allow your dog past the wire barrier. A long half-mile switchback helps tame the elevation gain.

Your dog will have a splendid time on these natural trails paying no heed to the history around her but there is the dam and remnants of the mill to investigate along the creek as well. The more you explore, however, the more challenge you inject into your dog's hiking day, which can be extended across the covered bridge and into Roswell's Old Mill Park.

Trail Sense: A trail map can be printed from the park website and mapboards are posted at critical trail junctions. There are unoffical foot-paths worn into the trail system from the surrounding neighborhoods.

Dog Friendliness

Dogs are permitted on the Vickery Creek Unit trails.

Traffic

No bikes, foot traffic only.

Canine Swimming

There are places for your dog to take a quick dip but Vickery Creek   access is not a goal of this trail system.

Trail Time

More than an hour.

31
Fort Yargo State Park

The Park

In the early 1790s the brothers Humphrey constructed four wooden forts to protect settlers moving into the area from Cherokee and Creek Indians who objected to the intrusion. Fort Yargo was one of the necklace of blockhouses that were more symbols of preparedness than hotbeds of activity. In 1810 David Humphreys sold Fort Yargo and 121 acres to John Hill for $167 to farm. In 1927 the forgotten blockhouse caught the attention of preservationists and in 1967 it was moved a short distance to this site and reassembled as the focal point for an 1,800-acre state park.

Barrow County

Phone Number
- (770) 867-3489

Website
- gastateparks.org/FortYargo

Admission Fee
- $5 parking fee

Park Hours
- 7 AM - 10 PM daily

Directions
- *Winder*, 210 South Broad Street, south of town. From Route 29/316, go north on Highway 81 to the park entrance on the right.

The Walks

There is plenty of canine hiking on tap at Fort Yargo - about 20 miles worth, but not many options. There are two trails around the park lake: the 12-mile, blue-blazed *Mountain Bike Loop* and the 7-mile, yellow-blazed *Lake Loop Trail*. Unless you are planning to turn your dog around after a short go of it, you will be locked into a multi-hour canine hike at Fort Yargo until you complete your circumnavigation of the 260-acre lake. It is an easy trot for your dog, however, as the *Lake Loop* drops in and out of the woods. The route serves up water views for long stretches, especially around the southern end. If you sample the rollercoaster bike trail with your dog, be aware that riders are required to ride in the same direction depending on the day of the week so you can walk in the opposite direction to see bikes coming.

Fort Yargo is one of America's best-preserved 18th-century blockhouses.

Trail Sense: There are mapboards, a trail map on the website and the trails are well-marked.

Dog Friendliness

Dogs are allowed on the trails and in the campground - one of the three cottages is dog-friendly but none of the yurts. Dogs are not allowed on the swimming beach.

Traffic

Bikes are allowed on the _Recreational Trail_ as well as the _Mountain Bike Trail_.

Canine Swimming

Your dog should be able to find a spot to slip into the lake at some point.

Trail Time

This is not the place for a quick jaunt for your dog - expect to spend about three hours once you start around the lake.

32
Brasstown Bald

The Park

With a summit elevation of 4,784 feet, Brasstown Bald is the highest point in Georgia. The name derives not from a thriving metal industry in the area but from a bungled translation of a Cherokee Indian word. The Cherokees embraced a legend that explained treeless mountaintops like this one - the forests were cleared to expose the presence of a great, winged monster harassing their villages which allowed their Great Spirit to slay the menacing beast.

The Walks

There is only one way for your dog to tag the summit of Brasstown Bald - straight up a steep, paved path for a half-mile that gains 100 feet of elevation for every 500 feet hiked. At the summit your dog will join the throngs who instead took the shuttle bus from the parking lot to the stone interpretive center on the mountaintop. Your dog's reward for this exhortation is a 360-degree view that takes in four states and even the Atlanta skyline on a crisp day.

Brasstown Bald is not a grassy peak but instead shrouded with a mix of Rosebay and Catawba rhododendron peppering a gnarly dwarf forest of twisted red oak and white oak. As such there are no real views until your dog clambers up the final steps of the observation deck.

For canine hikers who don't feel a half-mile hike, regardless of how vigorous, is sufficient to claim to have tagged a mountain, there are longer

Union County

Phone Number
- (706) 754-6221

Website
- fs.usda.gov/conf

Admission Fee
- Parking fee

Park Hours
- Sunrise to sunset; the facilities close in the winter but the summit is open as long as the weather is good and GA Spur 180 is open.

Directions
- *Chattahoochee National Forest*; southeast of Blairsville. Go south on US 19/129 for 8 miles and turn left (east) onto GA 180. Turn left on GA Spur 180 after 9 miles. Go 3 miles up the road to the parking lot.

approaches from deep in the Brasstown Bald Wilderness. Parking is limited at these trailheads and all of the hikes are of the out-and-back variety. The *Wagon Train Trail* was intended as GA 66 and is the least severe as it approaches from seven miles away at Young Harris. *Jack's Knob Trail* rises from the *Appalachian Trail* 4.5 miles to the south and the *Arkaquah Trail* crosses the ridgetop from the west.

Four states sprawl beneath your dog once he reaches the summit of Brasstown Bald.

All gain at least 1,800 feet in elevation and all end at the Brasstown Bald parking lot - from which you still need to hike up that paved access trail to reach the roof of Georgia.

Trail Sense: All the trails radiate from the Brasstown parking lot so finding the trailheads will be your main concern.

Dog Friendliness

Dogs are welcome on the Brasstown Bald summit but not in the Visitor Center.

Traffic

Foot traffic and shuttle buses to the summit.

Canine Swimming

None.

Trail Time

A full day if you are tagging the summit from the Brasstown Bald Wilderness.

33
Cooper Creek
Recreation Area

The Park

Chances are if you have made your way to the 1,240-acre Cooper Creek Scenic Area you are in search of trout or big trees. The rainbows and brookies are hiding in the cold mountain waters of Cooper Creek and nearby Mulky Creek. The towering trees are yellow poplars and hemlocks and white pines growing at the southern tip of their range.

The Walks

This is actually more like "canine exploring" than "canine hiking." The trails in the Cooper Creek Scenic Area are oft times, in the words of Ghostbuster Dr. Peter Venkman, "more of a guideline than a rule." At the main parking lot on FS 236 at the Cooper Creek bridge, you can cross the road and the slender Tom Jones Branch and launch a canine hike on the barely defined *Eyes on Wildlife Trail*. The 1.5-mile loop that easily gains its 200 feet is characteristically dark under the thick groves of hemlocks and white pines. On the parking lot side of the road there is no defined trail at all but your dog can trot down down lanes made by fishermen.

The tallest trees in the Scenic Area, where an estimated 100 acres of old-growth cove hardwoods are estimated to survive south of Cooper Creek, is not penetrated by any formal trails at all, but by a series of old roadbeds. The exploration begins off FS 33 and about one mile down the road you will reach the thickest tree in the entire Chattahoochee National Forest - a tulip poplar measuring more than 18 feet around. Another quarter-mile

Union County

Phone Number
- (706) 754-6221

Website
- fs.usda.gov/conf

Admission Fee
- None

Park Hours
- Sunrise to sunset

Directions
- *Chattahoochee National Forest*; northwest of Dahlonega. Follow GA 60 for 26 miles and turn right on Forest Service Road 4. The campgrounds and trailheads are six miles in. From Blue Ridge take GA 60 for 15.5 miles and turn left on Forest Service Road 4.

will land you in the "Valley of the Giants."

The most popular trails at Cooper Creek are on the north side near the campground where the *Mill Shoals, Cooper Creek* and *Yellow Mountain* trails conspire to form about a six-mile canine hiking loop. Although you are heading to the top of Yellow Mountain an athletic dog will scarcely be taxed by the effort.

Trail Sense: The National Forest Service blazes all its recreation areas with lime green markings which don't inspire great confidence without the context of a map so make sure you have one or arrive fired with the spirit of the explorer.

Dog Friendliness
Dogs are welcome on the trails and in the campgrounds.
Traffic
No horses and no bikes.
Canine Swimming
Your dog can join the trout in the streams when no anglers are present.
Trail Time
A couple hours to a full day.

34
ᵫs H. (Sloppy) Floyd State Park

The Park

This area was managed as a public fishing area until it was designated as the 169-acre Chattooga Lakes State Park in 1973. A year later the park was dedicated in the memory of James H. "Sloppy" Floyd, a member of the Georgia House of Representatives from 1953 until his death in 1974. Floyd, head of the Georgia House Appropriations Committee, hailed from nearby Trion. In the 1990s an additional 276 acres were purchased from Georgia Marble and today two of the prime attractions of the park are still the fishing lakes and an undeveloped marble mine.

Chattooga County

Phone Number
- (770) 975-0055

Website
- gastateparks.org/JamesHFloyd

Admission Fee
- $5 parking fee

Park Hours
- 7 AM - 10 PM

Directions
- *Summersville*; southeast of town. From I-75 take Exit 306 west through Adairsville on GA140. Turn right on US 27 and follow to the park entrance.

The Walks

At Floyd State Park your dog can indulge in some of his laziest trotting or dial up the Challenge-o-Meter to 10. You can begin with an amble along the Lower and Upper lakes and then set off on the .8-mile trek up to the Marble Mine. This journey travels on a rough

Your dog won't find more tranquil hiking in Georgia than lakeside at Floyd State Park.

and rutted old road that features a hard pull over the final 200 yards. Your dog can cool off after the spirited climb in a small pool at the mine, fed by a

Bonus

If your dog enjoys poking around the park trails and the _Pinhoti Trail_ along Taylor's Ridge you may want to consider signing up for the Twisted Ankle Trail Marathon/ Half Marathon that is staged here every May.

Marble Mine is the favored destination for canine hikers in James H. (Sloppy) Floyd State Park.

seasonal waterfall. You can return down the same road or circle to the right and complete a short loop at the base of Taylor's Ridge.

The Marble Mine can also be your jumping off point to the _Pinhoti Trail_ (a Creek Indian word meaning "turkey home") that crosses Taylor's Ridge as part of its 335-mile run through Alabama and Georgia. To reach that ridgeline requires a slog up "Becky's Bluff" that gains 700 feet in elevation in less than a mile. Your dog's four-wheel drive will be an asset here.

Trail Sense: The trail junction signs and park map should keep you oriented in Floyd State Park.

Dog Friendliness
Dogs are allowed on the park trails and in the campground.

Traffic
Foot traffic only and there is not a great deal of competition for these trails.

Canine Swimming
There is easy access to the lakes for canine aquatics as long as you don't disturb the fishermen.

Trail Time
Anywhere from 45 minutes to a full day.

35
Pickett's Mill Battlefield Historic Site

The Park

Union General William T. Sherman's plan to capture the prize of Atlanta in the Civil War was predicated on abandoning the railroad supply line through Allatoona Pass and outflanking the Confederate defenses. This movement south in late May of 1864 landed his army in a thickly forested wilderness striped with only rough, narrow roads. As the Rebel forces maneuvered to block his path the Union Army was hindered by constant skirmishing and three major battles at New Hope Church, Dallas and here, along a branch of the Pumpkinvine Creek where Malachi Pickett's family owned a grist mill.

In five hours of oft-times confused nocturnal fighting the Federal attack failed to dislodge entrenched Confederate forces and were driven from the field with the loss of over 1,600 troops from a 14,000-man force. The Southerners loss was placed at 500. The Battle of Pickett's Mill was a decisive Confederate victory but only delayed Sherman's capture of Atlanta by about a week. In his memoirs Sherman did not even see fit to mention the engagement at Pickett's Mill in his description of the Atlanta Campaign. Today the battlefield is one of America's best preserved Civil War sites but that is mostly serendipity rather than reverent planning. There was almost no interest in Pickett's Mill for 100 years. For owner Georgia Kraft Company the land was just more of its faceless million acres of timberland until

Paulding County

Phone Number
- (770) 443-7850

Website
- georgiastateparks.org/ PickettsMillBattlefield

Admission Fee
- Yes, paid in the Visitor Center through which you must pass with your dog.

Park Hours
- Budget constraints have currently limited hours to 9-5, Thursday through Saturday only

Directions
- *Dallas*; northeast of town. From Exit 277 of I-75 follow GA 92 west as it becomes Dallas-Acworth Road. Turn left on Mt. Tabor Church to the park entrance on the left. Various routes are well-marked with brown directional signs.

preservation-minded citizens convinced the State of Georgia to purchase the property and establish a state historic site in 1973.

The Walks

With its yawning ravines, gurgling brooks and pleasing woodlands these well-groomed four miles of trails would be a magnet for canine hikers even without their historical significance. Your dog will trot easily along roads used by troops on both sides and past well-preserved earthworks as several trails trace the movements of the armies. Several steep passages on the property will illuminate the desperate circumstances for those trapped here in 1864.

Trail Sense: Maps and interpretive signs lead the way.

Dog Friendliness
Dogs are welcome to explore the battlefield.
Traffic
Foot travel only.
Canine Swimming
The streams are seldom deep enough for anything more than a refreshing splash.
Trail Time
Allow more than an hour to fully absorb the events the Battle of Pickett's Mill.

36
Chattahoochee River NRA-Johnson Ferry

The Park

James Vann, son of a Scots trader and a Cherokee woman, was one of the most colorful of early Atlanta characters. In addition to running the first ferry across the Chattahoochee River in 1804 he owned taverns, grist mills, and livestock. Vann was the richest man in the Cherokee Nation, owned a reported 100 slaves, had at least nine wives and sired over 30 children.

Flatboats became common over the ensuing decades at established fords where a man or woman could cross the Chattahoochee for a nickel. A full wagonload might cost a dollar. Johnson Garwood started his ferry service here in the 1820s. After the Civil War, bridge-building techniques became more advanced and less expensive and the ferries of the Chattahoochee faded out of existence.

Fulton County

Phone Number
- (678) 538-1200

Website
- nps.gov/chat

Admission Fee
- Parking fee

Park Hours
- Sunrise to sunset

Directions
- *Atlanta*; Take Exit 24 off I-285 and follow Riverside Drive north to Johnson Ferry Road. When it ends after 2.3 miles turn left and get in the right lane - the parking area is immediately across the river on the right.

The Walks

From the time you pull into the back parking lot that is fighting an onslaught of grass and your dog jumps out of the car, this is like hiking through a ghost park. There are old pipes to the side, crumbling structures in the trees, leaning benches, weary signs that no longer have relevance. Your dog will love it.

From the parking lot three threads of trail, including the old service road in the center, push northward between the Chattahoochee River and a low ridge. You'll cross through marshland and several creeks before the

Bonus
Johnson Ferry is an ideal put-in point to canoe the Chattahoochee River with your dog. Powers Island is three miles downstream and it is six miles to Paces Mill on the normally gentle rapids.

trails come together in less than a mile and you can amble back with your dog. If the easy trotting through the light woods at Johnson Ferry turns addictive you can continue your explorations south of Riverside Drive along the river.

Trail Sense: There is a mapboard in the parking lot which will get you started and a minute of study is all you will need.

Dog Friendliness
Dogs are welcome at Johnson Ferry.

Traffic
No bikes, foot traffic only.

Canine Swimming
The bank above the Chattahoochee River is often 10-15 feet above the water but there is an occasional small dirt beach for your dog. There is also a seasonal pool of water that collects just north of the parking lot that is ideal for some dog paddling.

Trail Time
Less than an hour; more if your dog is just looking for a relaxing stroll.

37
Cascade Springs
Nature Preserve

The Park

The peaceful woodlands of this passive-use city park belie a busy, and sometimes tumultuous past. In 1864 as General William Sherman sought to subdue Atlanta he focused on capturing the quartet of railroads supplying the town. One, the Atlanta & West Point, ran through these woods. Union troops under the command of John Schofield failed to dislodge entrenched Confederate troops in three days of skrimishing here in the Battle of Utoy Creek. An estimated 850 federal casualties were stacked against some 35 losses for the South. Sherman would make no mention of the setback at Utoy Creek in his memoirs, a rare Confederate success during the Atlanta Campaign.

Fifty years of inactivity ended in 1913 as the springs gurgling out of the hillsides were declared to have restorative properties. The waters were bottled and sold and Cascade Springs Resort opened with a hotel and lighted dance pavilion. The commercial enterprises dried up during the 1930s and the land resisted further development until the City acquired the property in 1978 and created the 120-acre Nature Preserve.

Fulton County

Phone Number
- None

Website
- None

Admission Fee
- None

Park Hours
- 7:30 AM-3:00 PM Mon-Fri
  7:30 AM-6:00 PM Sat-Sun
  (entrance is gated)

Directions
- *Atlanta*; 2852 Cascade Road, west of downtown. From I-285 take Exit 7 on Cascade Road to the park on the right.

A stone springhouse is a well-preserved souvenir from the days when Cascade Springs was a popular resort.

The Walks

Within minutes of pulling into the parking lot the surrounding strip malls and busy neighborhoods will disappear in the wooded hillsides at Cascade Springs. Your dog will bound easily up the slopes on narrow footpaths, always under cover of a towering hardwood forest. There are some three miles of natural trails in the Nature Preserve that slip past fading Civil War trenches and ruins of a pump house and a spring house.

Trail Sense: No maps and no blazes; after you descend the boardwalk and spill out across Turkeyfoot Creek follow the asphalt path to the right or left to access the trail around the park perimeter. You will encounter trail signs at junctions but with no reference point.

Dog Friendliness
This a popular spot for dogwalkers.

Traffic
Foot traffic only.

Canine Swimming
The creeks are deep enough only for splashing for the most part.

Trail Time
Canine hikes can range from a quick 15-minute spin to a full hour to circle the park completely.

The namesake cascades will provide a refreshing break for your trail dog on a steamy day.

38
Warwoman Dell
Recreation Area

The Park

The "warwoman" was a powerful Cherokee elder who held sway over local sachems in the matters of war. She is believed to have visited the Dell each spring to conduct tribal rituals. In 1775 36-year old William Bartram traveled through the Cherokee Nation here on an epic journey from the the foothills of the Appalachian mountains to Florida, and all the way to the Mississippi River, collecting specimens and sketching plants, establishing himself as America's first naturalist. He became the country's first nature writer in 1791 with the publication of *Travels*, an account of his adventure. In 1976 the Bartram Trail Conference was founded to develop recreational trails that commemorate the Philadelphia botanist's wanderings, a 37-mile stretch of which passes through Georgia and Warwoman Dell.

Radun County
Phone Number
- (706) 754-6221
Website
- fs.usda.gov/conf
Admission Fee
- None
Park Hours
- Sunrise to sunset
Directions
- *Chattahoochee National Forest*; three miles east of Clayton. In town, north of the intersection of Routes 441/23/15 with 76/2 take Rickman Road east. Turn right when it joins Warwoman Road and continue to the park on the right hand sign of the road at the sign on the left.

The Walks

The once denuded Dell is now thick with white oak and hickory shading a luxurious understory of rhododendron. Although small in area there is an abundance of spirited canine hiking here. A highlight destination is across Warwoman Road, out of the Dell, accessed from the parking lot along the *Bartram Trail* which switches quickly up the hillside to the roadway. The trail continues across the road with a short, frothy climb that will set your dog to panting - you are heading to Becky Branch Falls which will be seen from a wooden bridge. You can close the loop and return to Warwoman Dell on a

Forest Service trail that emerges 100 feet down the road from the *Bartram Trail* you enetered on. The entire trip is about a half-mile.

Back in the Dell the forest is explored on a .4-mile *Nature Trail* that travels partly on the graded roadbed of the former Blue Ridge Railroad that South Carolina Senator John C. Calhoun dreamed would connect Charleston with Chattanooga. The 195-mile railroad was chartered in 1852 but by 1859 only the section between Anderson and Walhalla in South Carolina had been put into operation. Substantial work had been done digging tunnels, including a tunnel four miles east of here at Dicks Creek but the Civil War interrupted progress. After the war nothing more was ever done and no trains ever rolled on the wide, flattened path where your dog happily trots today. The *Nature Trail* boasts its own waterfall and a set of weathered stone steps that are another souvenir of the area's railroading activity.

Trail Sense: There is a mapboard in the parking lot that will orient you through Warwoman Dell but there is no mention of Becky Branch Falls.

Dog Friendliness
Dogs are welcome in the Recreation Area and along the *Bartram Trail*.

Traffic
Foot travel only on the small trail system.

Canine Swimming
Your dog will find the energetic stream lubricating the Dell worthy only of splashing.

Trail Time
About one hour, with many more waiting on the *Bartram Trail*.

39
Hard Labor Creek State Park

The Park

The park's distinctive name comes from either the Creek Indians who found crossing the swift-moving shoals an onerous chore or from the slaves who toiled under a blistering sun in the cotton and corn fields here. Either way, the park is a result of the hard labor of the Civilian Conservation Corps that was part of President Franklin Roosevelt's "tree army" during the Great Depression. In 1934 the federal government bought up 44 parcels of land to create the Hard Labor Creek Recreational Demonstration Area to reclaim marginal farmland for recreation. The eroded cropland was stabilized and thousands of pine trees were planted, roads graded and lakebeds dug. In 1946, the 5,804-acre Recreation Demonstration Area was presented to the State of Georgia and became one of the system's largest parks.

Morgan County
Phone Number
- (706) 557-3001
Website
- gastateparks.org/info/hardlabor/
Admission Fee
- $5 parking fee
Park Hours
- 7:00 AM-10:00 PM Daily
Directions
- *Rutledge*; Fairplay Road. From I-20 take Exit 105 north into the small town of Rutledge. Follow signs onto Fairplay Road and continue three miles past town to the park.

The Walks

Hard Labor Creek features two connected nature loops on the west side of Lake Brantley that ramble easily through second-growth pine-oak woodlands. The *Brantley Trail* covers a few paw-lengths over a mile and drops into the bottomlands of a stream that feeds the lake. The namesake beaver pond and wetlands are the highlights of the 1.5-mile *Beaver Pond Trail* where the forestscape is recovering from a century of intensive cotton farming. The now-wooded slopes were once under heavy cultivation and scars from the damage are still evident.

The marquee trails in the park, however, are the 22 miles of equestrian trails, divided into two loops at Lake Rutledge and Lake Brantley. Canine hikers are permitted on the horse paths and cut-off trails make for more manageable hiking loops in the four-mile range. There are no grand destinations here as you roll past

granite outcroppings under the mixed pines and hardwoods; the reward is long, solitary hiking with your dog. Always give right-of-way to the horses on their trails.

Trail Sense: The red-blazed and yellow-blazed nature trails each have color co-ordinated descriptive brochures and a trail map is available.

Dog Friendliness

Dogs are not only allowed in the park and the campground but two cabins have been designated dog-friendly. Your dog may spend the night in the same cabin as Tatum O'Neal and Kristy McNichol did when they were romping with Matt Dillon in *Little Darlings* or where Jason came back to life in *Jason Lives: Friday the 13th Part VI*. Both movies filmed camp scenes at Hard Labor Creek State Park.

Traffic

Foot traffic only on the nature trails.

Canine Swimming

Lake Rutledge and Lake Brantley are ideal venues for a swim and a fetch.

Trail Time

About an hour on the hiking-only trails, a full day possible on the horse trails.

40
Morningside
Nature Preserve

The Park

These are part of the lands once controlled by Benjamin Plaster, an early settler in Atlanta. Plaster was born in North Carolina in 1780 and moved to Franklin County, Georgia in 1802. He served as a private in the War of 1812 and after mustering out arrived in the newly formed De Kalb County to be a planter. His will of 1836 is the oldest on record in the county and lists holdings of 1316 acres.

By the 21st century, when a group of neighborhood residents fought for three years to prevent the destruction of 30 acres of mature forest, the parkland was transferred to the City of Atlanta as the Wildwood Urban Forest. It was renamed the Morningside Nature Preserve.

De Kalb County

Phone Number
- None

Website
- http://174.37.215.145/
government/parks/morningside.aspx

Admission Fee
- None

Park Hours
- Sunrise to sunset

Directions
- *Atlanta*; 1941 Wellbourne Drive. Take Exit 88 from I-85 and travel south on Cheshire Bridge Road. Turn left on Wellbourne Drive to the park entrance.

The Walks

You put this trail in the North Georgia mountains and no one would notice it but in northeast Atlanta it is a wonderland for canine hikers. Your dog will bound along a ribbon of sandy loam that meanders through an urban hardwood forest flavored with pines, splash in the South Fork Peachtree Creek and even glimpse a skyscraper or two to remind him where he is. This is easy going for your dog as the elevation gain along the one-plus miles of looping trail is less than 100 feet, topping out on a wooded knoll in the northwest corner of the park. Along the way you'll pass some craggy rock formations and weave between a phalanx of hackberry and box elder.

Trail Sense: Morningside is marked well enough to negate the need to summon St. Bernards to your rescue.

Dog Friendliness
Dogs are welcome in Morningside Nature Preserve.

Traffic
The park is popular with dog walkers, joggers and a bike or two.

Canine Swimming
The streams are usually deep enough only for splashing; keep an eye out for a sandy shoal where your dog can dig and splash.

Trail Time
Less than an hour.

Chattahoochee Plantation, south of town; on Paper Mill Road off Johnson Ferry Road from Exit 24 of I-285, Riverside Drive.

This is the most popular of the urban national park's 14 riverside units. You can count on sharing the park's main loop with joggers, bikes - and plenty of other dogs. That basic loop is the widest hiking path in Atlanta and about two miles in length with additional side detours where you can lead your dog away from the multitudes. Mostly flat, the Cochran Shoals trail system slips through wetlands, visits the Chattahoochee River and alternates between grassy open patches and young forest. The wide path makes Cochran Shoals one of the best places to soak up a sunny day with your dog.

More adventurous canine hikers will want to point north into the Sope Creek Unit where several miles of natural surface trails spin around the ruins of the Marietta Paper Mill. You are actually taking your dog away from the Chattahoochee River here but its 11-mile tributary, Sope Creek, does a fine job of standing in for the missing river and tree-ringed Sibley Pond makes a splendid canine swimming hole. The track is sportier and the crowds much less than Cochran Shoals, but the trails are favored by mountain bikers.

42
Big Trees Forest Preserve
Fulton County
Sandy Springs, at 7645 Roswell Road; north of town on the east side of Roswell Road (Route 9), four miles north of Exit 25 off I-285.

After pushing back against encroaching office complexes and shopping centers for decades this 30-acre urban forest was formally protected by a coalition of public and private activists in the early 1990s. Dogs are welcome sunrise to sunset in this leafy oasis and poop bags are provided. You won't ever escape the nearby traffic noise but your dog won't likely mind on the nearly two miles of wide, wood-mulched walking trails that ascend to a ridge and swing back along the attractive Powers Branch stream where the pools may be deep enough for small dogs to enjoy a swim. The "big trees" are mostly oaks (the pine trees are back in the parking lot) and some of the ancient survivors witnessed the Civil War.

43
Elachee Nature Science Center

Hall County

In Gainesville at 2125 Elachee Drive, off GA 13 (Atlanta Highway), north of Exit 17 from I-985.

The 1,500 acres of the Chicopee Woods Area Park, part of the easement held by the Elachee Nature Science Center, is one of the largest parks within city limits east of the Mississippi River. With some 13 miles of groomed trails the Center would surely rank higher on any list of canine hiking sites save for one thing - dogs are not permitted Monday through Friday from 9:00 a.m. to 3:00 p.m.

When you can get your dog on these trails, any type of hiking day is possible. Short trails wind through the scenic hardwoods and longer explorations await on the slopes of Chicopee Lake. One must-see destination at Elachee is the 140-foot suspension bridge that is one of fewer than a dozen suspension bridges in Georgia. Normally reserved for spanning deep gorges, this wooden one barely clears the head of an Irish Wolfhound. And while suspension footbridges often sway enough to intimidate a cautious dog from crossing, the Center's bridge is as sturdy as they come.

44
Lake Russell Wildlife Management Area

Stephens/Habersham County

West of Toccoa via GA 123; turn left on Route 184 towards Homer.

This chunk of the Chattahoochee National Forest encompasses about 17,000 acres, lubricated by the Middle Broad River. The federal government has been heavily involved in this land for 200 years. In the 1830s the Cherokee peoples were evicted from their villages here and after a century of tenant farming the U.S. Department of Agriculture showed up with a choice for residents: sell your farms to the government and move or have your property condemned and be evicted. In the years since forests and lakes have been rebuilt and grasslands re-established to stop erosion. Today the property is open to the public as a wildlife management area.

The Lake Russell WMA is a destination for canine hikers who love long rambles in the woods. The *Frady Branch Trails*, which use forest roads and footpaths, are designed for horses and mountain bikes and the entrance road into the 14-mile trail system is a full mile long. Once into the well-marked loops your dog will find the same rocky consistency on the trails as were on the roads. There are plenty of ups and downs but nothing too severe and a wealth of historic sites to visit, including family cemeteries, homesites and the flat stone remnants of a liquor still.

45
Murphey Candler Park
DeKalb County
At 1551 West Nancy Creek Drive east of Ashford Dunwoody Road, south of I-285, Exit 29.

The seeds for this park were sown in 1950 with the donation of 100 acres of land by Fred Wilson and 35 by Cora Quinn Long. When ground was broken on January 31, 1954 there wasn't even road access to the property - all the houses surrounding the park today were constructed after the park was created. The park was named for Charles Murphey Candler, a local politician.

The multi-use park is divided by Nancy Creek Drive and the north side is dominated by a lake which is circled by a 1.5-mile walking trail. You lose the lake after a quarter-mile on either side as you descend into wetlands and woodlands at the far end. But the reason to bring your dog to Murphey Candler is the best canine swimming in Atlanta from a dirt beach on the east side of the lake. Poop bags are provided in parking lots on either side of the lake.

You won't be able to wipe the wag off your dog's tail when she sees the dirt beach on the east side of the lake in Murphey-Candler Park.

46
Yellow River Park

Gwinnett County
At 3232 Juhan Road in Stone Mountain, off of Annistown Road.

The Yellow River rises in Gwinnett County and flows 78 miles to form the Ocmulgee River. As it passes through this heavily vegitated stretch the county has carved out a 566-acre park boasting a 12-mile trail system with separate routes for horses and bikes but most of the pedestrian trails are still on the drawing board. Still, canine hikers can use all the trails, not just the paved *Multi-Use Trail* which circles around an open area and along the riverbanks. If you venture onto the natural trails with your dog, the equestrian trails are a safer bet. The single-track bike trail gets narrower, hillier and more tightly routed the further you get from the trailhead.

47
Suwanee Creek Park

Gwinnett County
South of Suwanee at 1170 Buford Highway (Route 13/23).

Robert H. Allen settled here in 1867, five years before the town of Buford was organized. At first he ran a livery but soon he launched a little tanning business which his brother Bonaparte, who learned the tanning trade from their father Washington, took over in 1873 when he was 27. The Bona Allen Company started off making whiplashes and then horse collars and saddles, becoming one of the nation's biggest tanneries. Bona Allen crafted leather until 1981 but became famous for its hand-tooled saddles that were favored by many of Hollywood's most popular cowboy actors. In its more than 100 years of operation the tannery dumped enough chemicals and dyes into the Suwanee Creek that after it closed environmentalists estimated it would take another 100 years to return the waterway to health. Nature has proved much more resilient and the Suwanee is once again bristling with green wetlands and waterfowl, which are on display in the 84-acre park that is a terminus for the four-mile *Suwanee Greenway*. The thickly wooded park features a soft-surface path in addition to the paved *Greenway* that can be combined for a one-mile rollercoaster of a canine hike. If you venture down the *Greenway*, the adventure becomes tamer as you traverse the wooden walkways and hard-surfaced ribbons to reach George F. Pierce Park.

48

Oconee National Forest - Scull Shoals

Greene County

From I-20, take Exit 130 north on Route 44 into Greensboro; turn left on Route 15 and go north 12 miles to Macedonia Road on the right; turn and go two miles to Forest Road 1234 (gravel) on the left and follow two miles to Forest Road 1231 on the left. Turn and continue one mile to the parking area.

This land was settled by veterans of the Revolutionary War with land grants for their service and was the site of Fort Clark, a wooden blockhouse with stockade, in 1793 during the Oconee Indian War with the Creek Indians. Zachariah Sims and Thomas Ligon built mills on the Oconee River around 1800 and in 1810 operated the first paper mill in Georgia here. Scull Shoals developed into a prosperous agri-industrial community until a disastrous flood triggered by massive soil erosion from surrounding cotton farms inundated the community in 1887. In 1897 the mills were sold and the town abandoned and by 1935 when the federal government bought the land Scull Shoals was a ghost town.

The *Boarding House Trail* that explores the remains of Scull Shoals can seem as forgotten as the town itself as it visits the manager's house, the old power plant and the warehouse-store. Other nearby trails include the one-mile *Scull Shoals Trail* along the river and the *Indian Mounds Trail* at the end of Forest Service Road 1231A (passed on your left on the way in). Or you can take off with your dog for a hike down one of the lightly traveled forest roads.

The warehouse-store was once the hub of the Scull Shoals ghost town.

And because sometimes the best hikes with your dog do not take take place on dirt and grass...

49.
A Walking Tour of...
Downtown Atlanta

1. Underground Atlanta
Pryor Street and Alabama Street between Peachtree and Central streets

Until the advent of the railroad all the great cities of the world grew up in the immediate vicinity of a body of water. Atlanta did not; the town sprung from a surveyor's decision in 1837 after the State of Georgia decided it would construct its own railroad through the middle of the state to the Tennessee River and allow the proliferating private lines to link in to it. Atlanta grew around the Western and Atlantic Railroad and after the devastation of the Civil War the rebuilding began around the railroad tracks. Within fifty years Atlanta had become a very congested place. To better move the new horde of automobiles through the city a flurry of viaducts was constructed over the railroad tracks. Through the years as the city exploded above the viaducts the original trackside buildings became entombed along with the fortunes of the railroad. In the 1980s these abandoned structures were redeveloped into a nationally prominent retail and entertainment district. Under the Central Avenue viaduct, between Alabama and Wall streets can still be seen the original Zero Milepost of the the Western and Atlantic Railroad, inside one of the hundred-year old buildings. This isn't the exact location of the beginning of Atlanta but, after several trips around town, it is very close.

MAKE YOUR WAY TO THE
SURFACE AT ALABAMA
STREET AND CENTRAL AVENUE.

2. Georgia Railroad Freight Depot
Central Avenue and Alabama Street, adjacent to Underground Atlanta

This Italianate freight depot is the oldest standing structure in downtown Atlanta, constructed in 1869 to replace the Georgia Railroad station destroyed by Union troops in the Civil War. Architect Maxwell V.D. Corput, who landed many important commissions during the Reconstruction era, did this work for the railroad.

WITH YOUR BACK TO THE
DEPOT WALK THROUGH THE
PLAZA ALONG CENTRAL AVENUE
ON YOUR RIGHT TO THE CORNER
OF MARTIN LUTHER KING DRIVE.

3. Shrine of the Immaculate Conception
48 Martin Luther King Jr. Drive SE

Atlanta's first Catholic church, a wooden meetinghouse, was raised here in 1848. During the Civil War, Father Thomas O'Reilly, serving as pastor, interceded with Union troops to save this church and others from destruction. After the war the congregation moved the church to the back of the lot and began work on this Gothic-style brick church that was dedicated on December 10, 1873. In 1982, in the clean-up following a fire, the long-forgotten crypts of Father O'Reilly and another pastor, Thomas Cleary, were discovered under the main altar of the church. They rest there today.

TURN LEFT ON MARTIN
LUTHER KING DRIVE. TURN
RIGHT ON WASHINGTON
STREET.

4. Central Presbyterian Church
201 Washington Street

This is the second building to serve the congregation that was organized in 1858 with 39 members. The English Gothic style meetinghouse was crafted in 1885 of bricks with rough-hewn limestone used on the main facade. Stained glass, plaster and wainscoting inside are all original.

5. Georgia State Capitol
206 Washington Street

The capitol building was created in 1889 in the image of the United States Capitol as Atlanta was poised to assume the mantle as the "Capital of the New South." Architects Willoughby James Edbrooke and Franklin Pierce Burnham of Chicago provided the faithful rendition in Indiana limestone although plenty of native Georgia marble is in evidence inside. In 1958 the dome, surmounted by a female statue of Freedom, was covered in gold leaf from Dahlonega, Georgia. This site has historically been occupied by the government; Atlanta's first city hall was here before the land was donated to the state when Atlanta became the permanent capital in 1877.

TURN RIGHT ON
MITCHELL STREET.

6. Atlanta City Hall
68 Mitchell Street SW

Early in Atlanta's history if you needed to transact business with the town government you had to seek out officials in their offices in local hotels and grocery stores. In 1854 the first official city hall was constructed where the Georgia State Capitol stands today. When the state capital moved from Milledgville it actually did duty as the state capitol. That two-story brick structure was demolished in 1885.

The current City Hall came from the pen of Geoffrey Lloyd Preacher, a major figure in southeastern architectural history, in 1930. Preacher made his reputation with large-scale hotels but his creation of the elaborate Gothic-inspired Art Deco City Hall is probably his best known design. The building rises 14 stories with setbacks from the soaring, cathedral-like entrance. Preacher covered the reinforced concrete building with cream-colored terra cotta tiles.

In 1864 the home of Georgia attorney and jurist Richard Francis Lyon stood here when General William Sherman took it as his headquarters during the Union occupation of Atlanta. The house was one of the few that Federal troops did not destroy on the way to Savannah.

TURN RIGHT ON CENTRAL
AVENUE. TURN LEFT ON
MARTIN LUTHER KING DRIVE.

7. Fulton County Courthouse
160 Pryor Street, SW at Martin
Luther King Drive

Albert Anthony Ten Eyck Brown was born the son of an architect in 1878 in Albany, New York. Brown based his own practice in Atlanta where he became an important designer of public buildings. Here, in tandem with Thomas Morgan and John Robert Dillon, Brown created the largest courthouse in Georgia in 1914. The monumental granite Beaux Arts confection was also the first time Georgia ever spent more than a million dollars to build a courthouse.

CONTINUE TO FORSYTH STREET.

8. Martin Luther King Jr. Federal Building
77 Forsyth Street SW at southwest corner of Martin Luther King Drive

This splash of Art Deco came to the Atlanta streetscape in 1933 as the main city post office, courtesy of Depression-era funds. Albert Ten Eyck Brown provided the stripped-down classical design in contrast with his previous work at the county courthouse from twenty years earlier. In 1988 this became the first federal building to be named after the slain civil rights leader.

TURN RIGHT ON FORSYTH STREET. TURN LEFT ON MARIETTA STREET.

9. Walton Place (Georgia Railway and Power Building)
75 Marietta Street NW

Thomas Henry Morgan led Atlanta ever upward as a prominent architect at the beginning of the 20th century. This brick building with stone decoration was constructed in 1907 for the Georgia Railway and Power Company that began running streetcars in Atlanta in 1902.

10. Atlanta Journal Constitution Building
72 Marietta Street

The Atlanta Constitution put out its first editions in 1868 and within three years the upstart had run the more established Daily Intelligencer out of business, becoming the town's only newspaper. The Atlanta Journal began publishing in the evenings in 1883 and the two papers became fierce rivals, even after being yoked to the same corporate management when Ohioan James Middleton

Cox purchased the Constitution in 1950; he had bought the Journal eleven years earlier. The two papers merged into a single publication, Atlanta's only daily newspaper, in 2001. The papers operated from this nine-story office building from 1972 until it was donated to the city, along with a four-story printing press building, in 2010.

11. CNN Center
190 Marietta Street

In the 1970s Ted Turner took profits gleaned from his father's outdoor advertising firm and purchased an unpromising over-the-air UHF television station. He rented space on a communications satellite and transformed the little local station into America's first national "superstation." In 1980 Turner created the 24-hour news cycle by launching CNN, the first 24-hour news network. In 1987 Turner Broadcasting moved all its operations here, into a 1976 facility that had met with little success up to that point. The complex includes a company-owned Omni Hotel and is connected to the Philips Arena, home to the Atlanta Hawks of the National Basketball Association, a franchise Turner purchased in 1977.

WALK INTO THE PARK ACROSS MARIETTA STREET FROM THE CNN CENTER.

12. Centennial Olympic Park
Marietta Street at Centennial Olympic Park Drive NW

The 21-acre Centennial Olympic Park was created as the "town square" of the 1996 Olympic Games. The park retains several legacies to the Games including an interactive fountain in the shape of the Olympic Rings, symbolic Olympic torch columns and a statue of Pierre de Coubertin, father of the modern Olympic movement.

EXIT THE PARK AT CENTENNIAL OLYMPIC PARK DRIVE AND LUCKIE STREET. WALK DOWN LUCKIE STREET.

13. The Tabernacle
152 Luckie Street NW

In 1898 a pastor from North Carolina, whose determination was matched only by his ambition, arrived in Atlanta to head the Third Baptist Church. Almost immediately Leonard Gaston Broughton set his sights on a massive new church near the center of town. Broughton's efforts led members to break away from the congregation and start their own church. When his Board of Deacons declined to buy the property he was eyeing Broughton bought it himself and gave it to the church. The cornerstone for "Broughton's Tabernacle" was laid in 1910 and plans by Chattanooga architect Reuben Harrison Hunt, who designed churches across the South, called for a church and three other buildings, including a hospital. Broughton was also a physician who started the Georgia Baptist Medical Center and nursing school here. The red brick church building trimmed in granite was constructed in the Neoclassical style with a monumental Ionic facade. The Third Baptist Church grew to over 4000 members as Reverend Broughton moved on to Knoxville, Tennessee. Through the 20th century the congregation dwindled until, with fewer than 100 members, the building was sold in 1994. In the years since it has been redeveloped into an acclaimed performance hall.

TURN LEFT ON SPRING STREET. TURN RIGHT ON CARNEGIE WAY. THE LARGE CIRCULAR TOWER ON YOUR LEFT IS...

14. Peachtree Plaza Hotel
210 Peachtree Street NW

The official Georgia Governor's Mansion was once located here. That Victorian house was brought down in the 1920s. This cylindrical glass tower came along in 1976 and was Atlanta's tallest building for a decade. When the Peachtree Plaza opened it was the tallest all-hotel skyscraper in the world and is still the second tallest hotel in America with more than 1,000 rooms under its 723-foot high roof.

TURN LEFT ON ELLIS STREET.

15. Carnegie Building
133 Carnegie Way at Ellis Street

This 12-story brick and limestone building began life on April 11, 1929 as the Wynne-Claughton Building. Morgan T. Wynne started his real estate career in Atlanta almost 40 years earlier in the 1890s and cleared the old Ewell Hotel for this office building. Architect G. Lloyd Preacher provided the Chicago Style skyscraper with a flurry of Beaux Arts decoration and distinctive curved corners to fit into the triangular building site. Most people came to know this as the Carnegie Building, only because it faced the Andrew Carnegie Library across the street. Even after the library was razed this was still called the Carnegie Building, although the one-time richest man in the world never had anything to do with it. Most recently it has been converted into a boutique hotel.

TURN RIGHT ON
PEACHTREE STREET.

16. Winecoff (Ellis) Hotel
176 Peachtree Street NW at
Ellis Street

William Lee Stoddart was an architect who made his career building high-rise urban hotels, often in mid-size cities where his buildings were the tallest in town. Stoddart's practice was in New York City but he married an Atlanta girl in 1898 and established an office in town from which he directed the construction of many hotels around the Southeast, including this one in 1913. The Winecoff became nationally known - in a tragic way - on December 7, 1946 when 119 people perished in a fire here. Several dozen guests leaped to their deaths from the 15-story tower in what remains the deadliest hotel fire in American history. At the time the building had neither fire escapes, fire doors, nor sprinklers. The disaster at the Winecoff brought about many changes in American building codes. The hotel reopened in 1951 as the Peachtree and spiraled downhill over the years into a residence for the elderly and then vacancy. It was restored as the Ellis Hotel in 2007.

ON YOUR RIGHT, AT AN ANGLE, WHERE CARNEGIE WAY AND BROAD STREET JOIN PEACHTREE STREET IS...

17. Atlanta-Fulton County Library
One Margaret Mitchell Square

The county library system launched in 1902 on the back of a grant from industrialist Andrew Carnegie, one of some 2,500 public libraries he funded. The building was replaced in 1980 with this cantilevered creation from Marcel Breuer, the last project completed by the 80-year old leader of the Modernist Movement.

18. Georgia-Pacific Tower
133 Peachtree Street NE

On this site once stood Loew's Grand Theater which had its roots in an 1893 performance house and where the world premiere of Gone with the Wind was held. The theater, designated an historic property, held its downtown site as its property value soared and its movie revenues collapsed through the 1960s and 1970s. The theater burned, some thinking all too conveniently, in 1978 and this million-square-foot-plus office tower rose in its stead. The stepped tower clad in Georgia pink marble was opened in 1982 on designs from Skidmore, Owings and Merrill, a Chicago architectural firm responsible for some of the tallest towers in the world. This headquarters for Georgia-Pacific was Atlanta's second tallest building for a spell. Georgia-Pacific, a leading pulp and paper company, was founded by Owen Robertson Cheatham in 1927 in Augusta as the Georgia Hardwood Lumber Company.

19. Rhodes-Haverty Building
134 Peachtree Street NW

Amos Giles Rhodes was born in 1850 in Henderson, Kentucky. Laying crossties for the Louisville & Nashville Railroad brought Rhodes to Atlanta in 1875. He was soon operating a small furniture store but most people in Atlanta were still too poor to afford his goods. Rhodes hit on the concept of weekly installment payments which revolutionized the rebuilding of the war-devastated

South and launched his own empire. Rhodes died in 1928 as this building was being planned for his company and fellow furniture magnate J.J. Haverty. When the 21-story building with Byzantine and Art Deco elements was completed in 1929 it was the tallest in Atlanta and would reign as the city's sky king for a quarter-century. The Neoclassical wrap at the base is a later addition; it is now a hotel.

20.   Candler Building
127 Peachtree Street NE

Asa Griggs Candler was 35 years old in 1887 when he pooled $2,300 from his drugstore and patent medicine sales to purchase a beverage formula from fellow druggist John Pemberton. By 1894 Candler was selling his Coca-Cola in bottles and by 1904 he was constructing the tallest and most modern office building in the city. Much of architect George E. Murphy's lively Beaux Arts details can still be seen on the century-old tower. The stonework was carved from north Georgia Amicalola marble, personally selected by Candler and Murphy.

21.   Woodruff Park
east side of Peachtree Street NE

This park opened in 1973 on land purchased and donated by Robert W. Woodruff, who headed Coca-Cola from 1923 until 1954. The park, that includes two fountains, a performance pavilion, and several monuments, was originally four acres but now covers six.

22.   Flatiron Building
84 Peachtree Street NW at
Broad Street and Luckie Street

Why waste a perfectly good sliver of land where Broad Street runs into Peachtree Street when you can erect a skyscraper there? And that is what Bradford Lee Gilbert did in 1897 with this 11-story classically inspired tower. Gilbert is credited with constructing the world's first steel-framed building in New York City in 1889. His narrow triangular landmark building here predates the similar and more famous Flatiron Building in New York City by five years. Originally called the English-American Building, this was the second skyscraper constructed in Atlanta, preceded only by the Equitable Building planned by high-rise pioneers Daniel Burnham and John Wellborn Root. When the Equitable was brought down in 1971 the Flatiron Building was left as the city's oldest heritage skyscraper.

TURN RIGHT ON LUCKIE STREET, IN FRONT OF THE FLAT IRON BUILDING.

23.   Rialto Center for the Arts
80 Forsyth Street at Luckie Street

The original Rialto opened in 1916 as the largest movie house in the Southeast and once boasted the biggest electric marquee found anywhere south of New York City. That building was torn down in 1962 and replaced with this Rialto which operated until 1989. It was later revived by Georgia State University as a performance venue.

TURN LEFT ON FORSYTH STREET.

24. Tuttle Federal Courthouse
56 Forsyth Street NW between
Poplar and Walton streets

For the better part of 150 years the only dealings most Americans had with the federal government was with the post office. This monumental Beaux Arts post office of rusticated Georgia granite that occupies a full downtown block was constructed in 1908. Rising five stories and with a loading dock crafted of cast iron and glass, this was the first million-dollar building in Atlanta. The heavy cornice makes the building's low roof invisible from the street. When looking at such a massive stone pile it is useful to remember that it is not a solid block - without a light court in the center in the days before air conditioning the occupants of any interior offices would probably suffocate were that the case. The post office moved on in 1931 and judicial business has dominated the building in the years since.

25. Healey Building
57 Forsyth Street NW

Thomas G. Healey moved south from Connecticut in 1846 and started making bricks. The bricks led to construction and then to real estate and following the destruction wrought by the Civil War Healey became one of Atlanta's wealthiest men. This skyscraper was raised by a Healey son, William, in 1913 and it would remain in the family until 1972. The 16-story tower, constructed of stone and highlighted by Neo-Gothic terra cotta tile, was planned as a block-filling two-tower project but the twin was never built. As it is, this building brought down the curtain on what is regarded as Atlanta's first skyscraper era from 1893 to 1918.

TURN LEFT ON WALTON STREET.

26. The Grant Building
44 Broad Street NW at
southwest corner of Walton Street

This heritage skyscraper of limestone and terra cotta is a rare 19th century survivor in downtown Atlanta. Its large windows set in a grid are emblematic of the nascent Chicago Style of high-rise architecture. The building was completely renovated in 1980.

27. Empire Building
35 Broad Street NW at southeast
corner of Walton Street

This was the city's first steel-frame skyscraper when constructed in 1901. For most of its 100+ years the building has done duty as a bank under a parade of different nameplates but each retained the opulent banking floor seen inside today. In the 1930s, in order to project an aura of security, the ground floors were given a Renaissance-style facelift in stone by architect Philip Trammell Shutze.

28. Muse's Building
52 Peachtree Street NW at northwest
corner of Walton Street

George Muse came with his family to Atlanta from rural Alabama in 1869. He was only 16 years old but responsible for his mother and five siblings. It would take until 1887 before he was able to open the George Muse Clothing Company. In 1921 he commissioned this seven-story building constructed on the site of a one-time Confederate arsenal. Muse's, "the fashion center of the South," would remain here until 1992; after the clothier departed the building was converted into loft apartments.

TURN RIGHT ON
PEACHTREE STREET.

29. William-Oliver Building
32 Peachtree Street NW

This Five Points property was purchased in 1877 by Thomas G. Healey when it contained the store of Thomas Kile. This historic spot was where Atlanta held its first municipal elections in 1848. William and Oliver were Healey's grandsons who developed this office building in 1930 for lawyers and business owners. The 16-story William Oliver Building was the first Atlanta skyscraper built completely in the Art Deco style and it remains the city standard-bearer for Deco. Francis Palmer Smith and Robert Smith Pringle had formed an architectural partnership in 1922 and built a reputation on classical mansions for Coca-Cola executives. This was their first foray into the stripped down classicism of Art Deco and they outfitted the building with flashy geometric patterning and stylized chevrons. The William-Oliver Building established Pringle and Smith as the go-to Deco architects in the town in the 1930s. In the 1990s the last commercial tenants exited the building and it was renovated into luxury lofts.

30. Murrell's Row
**east side of Peachtree Street
between Edgewood Avenue
and Marietta Street**

Atlantans picked up their first mail here in the store of George Washington Collier and the town's first mayor, Moses W. Formwalt, had a tin and sheet metal shop here. More often townsfolk came here for cockfights and a drink. The den of undesirables who lived here came to take their name from a Tennessee mur-derer named John A. Murrell. The notoriety of the district had begun to fade when Union torches leveled the area during the Civil War.

TURN LEFT ON EDGEWOOD
AVENUE, IN FRONT OF MURRELL'S
ROW.

31. Hurt Building
50 Hurt Plaza

Joel Hurt was born in a town named for his family in Alabama and came to Atlanta in 1875 where he organized the Atlanta Building and Loan Association, which he helmed for 32 years. Hurt built Atlanta's first electric street line and anchored it with the town's first skyscraper, the Equitable Building, in 1893. The flatiron-shaped Hurt Building, wedged into this building site in 1913, was one of the crowning achievements of Joel Hurt's career. The classically flavored building was designed by prominent New York architect J.E.R. Carpenter in the prototypical Chicago-style three-part fashion to replicate a Greek column with a defined base, a shaft of windows laid on a grid and an ornate cornice. Entry came through a rotunda at the point of the property. The first tenants moved in during 1913 but the building was fiddled with and not completely finished until 1926, the year that Joel Hurt died.

BEAR RIGHT OF THE HURT
BUILDING INTO HURT
PLAZA. TURN RIGHT ON
PEACHTREE CENTER AVENUE.
TURN RIGHT ON MARIETTA
STREET. TURN LEFT ON
PEACHTREE STREET.

32. State of Georgia Building
2 Peachtree Street NW

This was the tallest building in the Southeast when it was constructed as the headquarters for First National Bank of Atlanta in 1966; its antenna topping out at just a few inches shy of 600 feet. The International Style building of marble and aluminum incorporated parts of the bank's building from 1903. First Atlanta itself was incorporated into Wachovia and disappeared in the 1990s. Today the building trundles on as state office space.

CONTINUE A FEW MORE STEPS AND YOU WILL REACH THE TOUR STARTING POINT AT UNDERGROUND ATLANTA.

50.
A Walking Tour of...
Midtown Atlanta

1. Bank of America Plaza
600 Peachtree Street NE

When this 1,024-foot tower was constructed in 1992 for Nations-Bank it was the ninth tallest building in the world. Although it has now slipped out of the top 50 it remains the tallest building in America found outside of New York City or Chicago. Crowning the dark red granite-faced tower is an open-frame steel pyramid that tapers to an obelisk-like spire mimicking the shape of the Art Deco-inspired building. Much of the spire has been slathered in 23-karat gold leaf.

ACROSS PEACHTREE STREET ON THE SOUTHEAST CORNER OF NORTH AVENUE IS...

2. North Avenue Presbyterian Church
607 Peachtree Street Northeast

The North Avenue Presbyterian Church was established in 1898 as a church in the "suburbs" at the time. Architects Alexander Bruce and Thomas Henry Morgan delivered a Romanesque church rendered in gray Stone Mountain granite for the congregation which held its first services here on Thanksgiving Day 1900. Additional wings were added in the 1920s and the 1950s and the sloping terrain of the lot disguises the five stories of the church.

WALK NORTH ON PEACHTREE STREET, CROSSING NORTH AVENUE.

3.   Ponce de Leon Apartments
75 Ponce de Leon Avenue at
southeast corner of Peachtree Street

This has been called "the city's most famous intersection" and celebrated architect William Lee Stoddart created a grand apartment building worthy of its corner in 1913. The Ponce de Leon billed itself as "the South's most luxurious apartments" and the second through ninth floors contained only two nine-to-ten room apartments per floor. The city's first penthouse graced the apartment roof. With a dining room serving three meals a day and shops lining the street level, the Ponce de Leon was a city unto itself. Stoddart outfitted his symmetrical building with Beaux Arts details, many of which remain. The facade curves to follow the line of the trolley tracks that once ran out front defining what was at one time the northern edge of Atlanta.

4.   Georgian Terrace Hotel
659 Peachtree Street NE

This is the kind of hotel where Clark Gable, F Scott Fitzgerald, and Calvin Coolidge would sign the guest register. Architect William Lee Stoddart designed the Georgian Terrace two years before he tackled the Ponce de Leon across the street and he used the streets of Paris as his model. Executed in tan brick, marble and limestone, the hotel boasts turreted corners, floor-to-ceiling Palladian-styled windows and wide wrap-around columned terraces. Look up to see a fanciful cornice rendered in terra cotta. In the 1920s, Arthur Murray, who was then a student at Georgia Tech University, started teaching dance classes in the hotel's Grand Ballroom, lessons that would become the foundation

for America's most famous franchise of dance schools. In the 1970s that ballroom was converted into the Electric Ballroom and hosted the likes of Billy Joel, Bruce Springsteen, Patti Smith and Fleetwood Mac. In 1991, the hotel was converted into a luxury apartment building and a new 19-story wing, complete with a roof-top pool, was built to resemble the original 10-story, Beaux-Arts hotel. In 1997, the apartments were vacated and the property reopened as a luxury hotel.

5.   Fox Theatre
660 Peachtree Street NE

This building began life in the 1920s as the Yaarab Temple Shrine Mosque, decorated with Moorish onion domes and minuets. When the price tag started to outstrip their means, movie mogul William Fox stepped in to bail out the Shriners. The result was an atmospheric theater that transported movie-goers to an exotic Arabian desert night as they waited for the show to begin. The Fox Theatre could seat more than 4,000 for a performance and operated as a jewel in the Fox chain for decades. The movie palace met a familiar end in the 1970s, done in by suburban flight and television, but it escaped the wrecking ball and was rescued by Atlanta Landmarks, Inc.

6.   Hotel Indigo
683 Peachtree Street NE

This brick tower with a stone wrap at its base and Beaux Arts detailing opened in 1925 as the Cox-Carlton, a residential hotel for single men. This was the first of a handful of highrises designed in Atlanta by Francis Palmer Smith and Robert Smith Pringle who teamed up in

1922 and built numerous residences in Buckhead and Druid Hills. In addition to their landmark skyscrapers Pringle and Smith became noted for their work for Coca-Cola, designing bottling plants and mansions for company executives.

7. Evangelical Lutheran Church of the Redeemer
731 Peachtree Street NE

The Lutheran Church of the Redeemer was founded in 1903 with 39 members in the shadow of the Georgia State Capitol. It was the second Lutheran church in Atlanta, but the first English-speaking congregation. The Lutherans obtained this property in 1937 and the current sanctuary was raised in 1952. Crafted of Tennessee quartzite and Indiana limestone, the low-slung Gothic structure was designed by Harold Wagoner of Philadelphia. Today, the congregation is the largest Cathedral-style Lutheran church in the Southeast.

8. Saint Mark United Methodist Church
781 Peachtree Street NE

The First Methodist Church established the Peachtree Street Mission in 1872 when this area was outside the city limits. That mission was located in a house on the east side of Peachtree Street just north of what is now Eighth Street. The congregation moved to this site with the new century in 1900 and the cornerstone for this Gothic-flavored church was laid in 1902. Crafted of gray Stone Mountain granite, this is one of three extant churches designed by noted Atlanta architect Willis Franklin Denny. Despite a career of only eight years that ended with his death of pneumonia in 1905 at the age of

31, Denny was influential in bringing Atlanta architecture from the picturesque Victorian era into the age of historically accurate revival styles.

9. Peachtree Manor Apartments
826 Peachtree Street NE

Georgia native Philip Trammell Shutze, who became the go-to architect for a wide range of projects in Atlanta in the first half of the 20th century, benefitted from several years of training in Italy early in his career. This brick Georgian Revival apartment house from 1923 was one of his earlier designs. Despite decades of neglect the stone details have survived in good order, including the rusticated Peachtree entranceway with "696 Peachtree" carved into it, a souvenir from the renumbering of Atlanta's main artery. Walk around the 6th Street side of the building to see the U-shape of Peachtree Manor, necessary to bring light and air into bulky buildings like this in the days before air conditioning.

10. Palmer House/Phelan Court Apartments
952 Peachtree Street NE at Peachtree Place

Sidney H. Phelan came from Alabama after the Civil War and made his money in the cotton business before turning his energies to development. On his homesite here he constructed two apartment buildings, one named for himself and the other for his wife, Palmer Graham. Phelan used Atlanta's top architects for his buildings. The town's leading Victorian architect, Gottfried Norman, designed the eclectic Flemish Revival Palmer Apartments along Peachtree Plaza (around the corner) in 1908. It stands today as one of Norman's few remaining buildings functioning in its original role. The Phelan Apartments were developed after Sidney Phelan's death in 1913 at the age of sixty. Norman was also not around for the new project, having committed suicide several years earlier. His successors Hal Hentz and Neel Reid worked on the plans. Also contributing design details was Philip T. Shutze who would become one of the leading architects in the Southeast over the next forty years. The elaborate classical doorway on the Peachtree Street facade is a Reid trademark.

11. Margaret Mitchell House
990 Peachtree Street NE

This building was known as the Crescent Apartments when Margaret Mitchell and her husband John Marsh lived in Unit #1 the 1920s. Mitchell, who worked as a newspaper reporter, would scarcely recognize the restored 1899 Victorian building today; she called the place "The Dump." By the time the Marshes moved out in 1932 only one other apartment in the run-down nine-unit building was occupied. It was in this house that Mitchell wrote most of the manuscript for Gone with the Wind and that is the reason this building was never razed, like nearly every other home in the neighborhood. Mitchell would be killed in 1949 at the age of 48 by a reckless driver while she was crossing Peachtree Street three blocks north of here.

TURN LEFT ON 10TH STREET AND HEAD TOWARDS WEST PEACHTREE STREET. AS YOU WALK, THE TOWER VISIBLE ON YOUR RIGHT IS...

12. One Atlantic Center
1201 West Peachtree Street NW

When this 820-foot tower was completed in 1987 as a regional headquarters for IBM, it was the tallest building in the Southeast. Its arrival triggered the rebirth of Midtown Atlanta as its pyramidal top served as a beacon for new development. The building is dressed in Spanish pink granite and sports Gothic flourishes, especially as it rises to its crown, which is topped by a gold peak.

TURN LEFT ON WEST
PEACHTREE STREET NW.

13. Academy of Medicine
875 West Peachtree Street NW

Science-oriented medicine in Atlanta traces its roots back to before the Civil War when the town wasn't even ten years old. In 1854 the Atlanta Medical College and the Brotherhood of Physicians, soon after known as the Atlanta Medical Society, was organized to discuss medical techniques and practices. The Academy led a peripatetic existence around town before moving into this Neoclassical home in 1941. The beautifully proportioned, temple-fronted building is another design by the acclaimed Philip T. Shutze.

14. Atlanta Biltmore Hotel and
Biltmore Apartments
30 5th Street at West
Peachtree Street NW

The proliferation of the automobile untethered grand hotels from America's train stations and downtowns in the 1920s and nowhere is there a better example than the block-swallowing Atlanta Biltmore. The local point man for the six-million dollar hotel was William Candler, son of Coca-Cola magnate Asa Candler, who developed the complex in association with the New York-based Biltmore hotel chain. The Neo-Georgian red brick hotel opened with great fanfare in 1924 with a symbolic parade of 1,000 cars making a sweep around the property. Beginning in 1925, WSB, the South's first radio station, broadcasted for more than 30 years from its studios on the top floor and the illuminated radio towers on the roof spelling out "BILT-MORE" became landmarks on the city skyline. Like most of its grand urban hotel cousins the Biltmore suffered spells of neglect, ownership shifts and vacancy. Extensive renovations came along in the 1990s.

15. AT&T Midtown Center
675 West Peachtree Street NW

Southern Bell erected the town's third tallest building for its headquarters in 1982. Architects Skidmore, Owings and Merrill of Chicago, known for their facility with tall towers, provided the plans. The building took a star turn in RoboCop 3, standing in for the futuristic Detroit headquarters of the evil mega corporation O.C.P. Most of the buildings seen in the film were slated for demolition to make way for facilities for the upcoming 1996 Olympics.

16. All Saints Episcopal Church of Atlanta
634 West Peachtree Street NW at northwest corner of North Avenue

Mary Jane Peters, whose husband Richard owned and developed most of land of today's Midtown, donated this land to the Diocese of Georgia in 1901 for "church purposes." The first chapel here was a wood and stucco affair designed by Harriett Dozier, a pioneering woman architect. The present sanctuary was dedicated on Palm Sunday 1906 and sprung from the pens of Thomas Henry Morgan and John R. Dillon, who donated their services.

TURN LEFT ON NORTH AVENUE.

17. Fire Station 11
30 North Avenue NE

Alexander Bruce and Thomas Henry Morgan were Georgia's leading architectural firm of the late 1800s. They were responsible for scores of public buildings, including this brick firehouse in 1907. The Station #11 Company was the first to respond to the fire in the Winecoff Hotel down Peachtree Street in 1946 that remains the worst hotel fire in American history to this day, claiming 119 lives. Many died leaping from the blazing hotel's upper floors. Today the century-old building has been adapted as a restaurant.

WALK ACROSS THE STREET TO BANK OF AMERICA PLAZA AND THE START OF THE WALKING TOUR.

Alphabetical Index to Parks Around Atlanta...

Other Books On Hiking With Your Dog from Cruden Bay Books
www.hikewithyourdog.com

DOGGIN' AMERICA: 100 Ideas For Great Vacations To Take With Your Dog - $19.95

DOGGIN' THE MID-ATLANTIC: 400 Tail-Friendly Parks To Hike With Your Dog In New Jersey, Pennsylvania, Delaware, Maryland and Northern Virginia - $18.95

DOGGIN' CLEVELAND: The 50 Best Places To Hike With Your Dog In Northeast Ohio - $12.95

DOGGIN' PITTSBURGH: The 50 Best Places To Hike With Your Dog In Southeast Pennsylvania - $12.95

DOGGIN' ORLANDO: The 30 Best Places To Hike With Your Dog in Central Florida - $9.95

DOGGIN' NORTHWEST FLORIDA: The 50 Best Places To Hike With Your Dog In The Panhandle - $12.95

DOGGIN' ASHEVILLE: The 30 Best Places To Hike With Your Dog in Western Carolina - $9.95

DOGGIN' THE POCONOS: The 33 Best Places To Hike With Your Dog In Pennsylvania's Northeast Mountains - $9.95

DOGGIN' THE BERKSHIRES: The 33 Best Places To Hike With Your Dog In Western Massachusetts - $9.95

DOGGIN' NORTHERN VIRGINIA: The 50 Best Places To Hike With Your Dog In NOVA - $9.95

DOGGIN' DELAWARE: The 40 Best Places To Hike With Your Dog In The First State - $9.95

DOGGIN' MARYLAND: The 100 Best Places To Hike With Your Dog In The Free State - $12.95

DOGGIN' JERSEY: The 100 Best Places To Hike With Your Dog In The Garden State - $12.95

DOGGIN' RHODE ISLAND: The 25 Best Places To Hike With Your Dog In The Ocean State - $7.95

DOGGIN' MASSACHUSETTS: The 100 Best Places To Hike With Your Dog in the Bay State - $12.95

DOGGIN' CONNECTICUT: The 57 Best Places To Hike With Your Dog In The Nutmeg State - $12.95

DOGGIN' THE FINGER LAKES: The 50 Best Places To Hike With Your Dog - $12.95

DOGGIN' LONG ISLAND: The 30 Best Places To Hike With Your Dog In New York's Playground - $9.95

DOGGIN' THE TIDEWATER: The 33 Best Places To Hike With Your Dog from the Northern Neck to Virginia Beach - $9.95

DOGGIN' THE CAROLINA COASTS: The 50 Best Places To Hike With Your Dog Along The North Carolina And South Carolina Shores - $11.95

DOGGIN' AMERICA'S BEACHES: A Traveler's Guide To Dog-Friendly Beaches - $12.95

THE CANINE HIKER'S BIBLE - $19.95

A Bark In The Park: The 55 Best Places To Hike With Your Dog In The Philadelphia Region - $12.95

A Bark In The Park: The 50 Best Places To Hike With Your Dog In The Baltimore Region - $12.95

A Bark In The Park: The 37 Best Places To Hike With Your Dog In Pennsylvania Dutch Country - $9.95

Made in the USA
Middletown, DE
04 December 2015